veggie food

veggie food

Kay Scarlett

LAUREL
GLEN

San Diego, California

Contents

Starters

Bruschetta

Classic Tuscan
6 ripe Roma tomatoes
$1/2$ cup basil, shredded
1 garlic clove, finely chopped
2 tablespoons extra-virgin olive oil

Mushroom and parsley
2 tablespoons olive oil
2 cups small button mushrooms,
    quartered
1 tablespoon lemon juice
$1^3/4$ oz. goat cheese, crumbled
1 tablespoon finely chopped
    Italian parsley
1 teaspoon chopped thyme

16 slices crusty white bread, cut
    into $1/2$-inch slices
4 garlic cloves, halved
$1/4$ cup olive oil

To make the classic Tuscan topping, score a cross in the base of each tomato, place the tomato in a bowl of boiling water for 10 seconds, then plunge it into cold water. Peel the skin away from the cross. Cut in half and scoop out the seeds with a teaspoon. Finely dice the flesh, then combine with the basil, garlic, and oil.

To make the mushroom and parsley topping, heat the oil in a frying pan and cook the mushrooms over medium heat for 5 minutes or until just tender. Remove from the heat and transfer to a small bowl. Stir in the lemon juice, goat cheese, parsley, and thyme.

Toast the bread, and while still hot, rub with the cut side of a garlic clove. Drizzle some olive oil over each slice of bread, then season with salt and freshly ground black pepper. Divide the toppings among the bread slices.

Serves 8

Note: Each topping makes enough for eight slices of bruschetta. You will only need eight slices of bread if you only want to make one topping.

Grilled asparagus with salsa

3 eggs
2 tablespoons milk
1 tablespoon olive oil
2 ears of corn
1 small red onion, diced
1 red pepper, finely chopped
2 tablespoons chopped thyme
2 tablespoons olive oil, extra
2 tablespoons balsamic vinegar
24 fresh asparagus spears
1 tablespoon macadamia oil
toasted whole-wheat bread, to serve

Beat the eggs and milk together. Heat the oil in a nonstick frying pan over medium heat, add the egg, and cook until just set. Flip and cook the other side. Remove and allow to cool, then roll up and cut into thin slices.

Cook the corn in a grill pan or in boiling water until tender. Allow to cool slightly, then slice off the corn kernels. Make the salsa by gently combining the corn, onion, pepper, thyme, extra olive oil, and balsamic vinegar.

Trim off any woody ends from the asparagus spears, lightly brush with macadamia oil, and cook in a grill pan until tender.

Serve the asparagus topped with a little salsa and the finely shredded egg, accompanied by fingers of buttered, toasted whole-wheat bread.

Serves 4–6

Carrot timbales with creamy saffron and leek sauce

4 tablespoons butter
2 leeks, sliced
2 garlic cloves, crushed
5 cups sliced carrots
1 1/2 cups vegetable stock
1 1/2 tablespoons finely chopped
  sage
1/4 cup cream
4 eggs, lightly beaten

Saffron and leek sauce
3 tablespoons butter
1 small leek, finely sliced
1 large garlic clove, crushed
1/4 cup white wine
pinch of saffron threads
1/3 cup crème fraîche

Preheat the oven to 325°F. Lightly grease six 3/4-cup timbale molds. Heat the butter in a saucepan over medium heat, add the leek, and cook for 3–4 minutes or until soft. Add the garlic and carrots and cook for 2–3 minutes. Pour in the stock and 2 cups water, bring to a boil, then reduce the heat and simmer, covered, for 5 minutes or until the carrots are tender. Strain, reserving 3/4 cup of the liquid.

Blend the carrots, 1/2 cup of the reserved liquid, and the sage until smooth. Cool slightly. Stir in the cream and egg, season with salt and pepper, and pour into the molds. Place the molds in a roasting pan filled with enough hot water to come halfway up the sides of the molds. Bake for 30–40 minutes or until just set.

To make the sauce, melt the butter in a saucepan and cook the leek over medium heat for 3–4 minutes without browning. Add the garlic and cook for 30 seconds. Add the wine, the rest of the reserved liquid, and saffron and simmer for 5 minutes or until reduced. Stir in the crème fraîche.

Invert the timbales onto serving plates and serve with the sauce.

Serves 6

Roasted field mushrooms with tarragon and lemon crème fraîche

⅓ cup olive oil
2 tablespoons lemon juice
4 garlic cloves, crushed
12 large, flat field mushrooms, brushed and stems trimmed
2 tablespoons finely chopped Italian parsley
toasted bread, to serve

Lemon crème fraîche
¼ cup crème fraîche
2 teaspoons lemon juice
1 garlic clove, crushed
2 teaspoons chopped tarragon

Preheat the oven to 400°F. In a large roasting pan, combine the oil, lemon juice, and garlic. Add the mushrooms and gently toss until coated. Season well with salt and pepper and arrange in a single layer. Roast for 30 minutes, turning several times to cook evenly.

In a small bowl, combine the crème fraîche, lemon juice, garlic, and tarragon.

Sprinkle the mushrooms and their cooking juices with parsley and serve with the lemon crème fraîche and toasted bread.

Serves 4

Mini leek pies

4 tablespoons butter
2 tablespoons olive oil
1 onion, finely chopped
3 leeks, finely sliced
1 garlic clove, chopped
1 tablespoon all-purpose flour
2 tablespoons sour cream
1 cup grated Parmesan cheese
1 teaspoon chopped thyme
4 sheets frozen puff pastry, thawed
1 egg, lightly beaten

Heat the butter and oil in a large frying pan over medium heat. Add the onion and cook, stirring occasionally, for 2 minutes. Add the leek and garlic and cook for 5 minutes or until the leek is softened and lightly browned. Add the flour and stir into the mixture for 1 minute. Add the sour cream and stir until slightly thickened. Transfer to a bowl and add the Parmesan and thyme. Season with salt and pepper and allow to cool.

Preheat the oven to 400°F. Place a lightly greased baking sheet in the oven to heat. Using a 2½-inch round cutter, cut the pastry into sixty-four circles. Place 2 heaping teaspoons of filling on half the pastry circles, leaving a small border. Lightly brush the edges with egg, then place another pastry circle on top. Seal the edges with a fork and lightly brush the tops with egg.

Place the pies on the heated baking sheet and bake for 25 minutes or until the pies are puffed and golden.

Makes 32

Tempura vegetables with wasabi mayonnaise

Wasabi mayonnaise
2 tablespoons mayonnaise
1 tablespoon wasabi paste
1/2 teaspoon grated lime zest

2 egg yolks
1 cup chilled club soda
1/4 cup cornstarch
1 cup all-purpose flour
1/4 cup sesame seeds, toasted
vegetable oil, for deep-frying
1 large eggplant (9 oz.), cut into
 thin rounds
1 large onion, cut into thin rounds
 with rings intact
2 medium orange sweet potatoes
 (10 1/2 oz.), cut into thin rounds

To make the wasabi mayonnaise, combine all the ingredients. Transfer to a serving bowl, cover with plastic wrap, and refrigerate.

Place the egg yolks and club soda in a bowl and mix lightly with a whisk. Sift the cornstarch and flour into a separate bowl. Add the sesame seeds and some salt and mix well. Pour the club soda and egg yolk mixture into the flour and stir lightly with a fork or chopsticks until just combined but still lumpy.

Fill a deep, heavy-based saucepan or wok one-third full of oil and heat until a cube of bread dropped into the oil browns in 15 seconds. Dip pairs of the vegetables—eggplant and onion or eggplant and sweet potato—into the batter and cook in batches for 3–4 minutes or until golden brown and cooked through. Drain on crumpled paper towels and season to taste with salt and pepper. Keep warm, but do not cover or the tempura coating will become soggy.

Transfer the tempura to a warmed serving platter and serve immediately with the wasabi mayonnaise.

Serves 4–6

Peppers rolled with goat cheese, basil, and capers

4 large red peppers
1/4 cup Italian parsley, chopped
2 tablespoons chives, chopped
2 tablespoons baby capers, finely chopped
1 tablespoon balsamic vinegar
5 1/2 oz. goat cheese
16 basil leaves
olive oil, to cover
crusty Italian bread, to serve

Cut the peppers into large, flat pieces and remove any seeds. Put them in a baking tray skin-side up and place under a broiler until the skin blisters and blackens. Place in a plastic bag and leave to cool, then peel away the skins. Cut into 1 1/4-inch-wide pieces.

Combine the parsley, chives, capers, and balsamic vinegar in a small bowl. Crumble in the goat cheese and mix well. Season with lots of pepper. Place a basil leaf on the inside of each pepper piece and top with a teaspoon of the goat cheese mixture. Fold the pepper over the cheese and secure with a toothpick. Place in an airtight, nonreactive container and cover with olive oil. Refrigerate until ready to serve. Allow to return to room temperature before serving with crusty Italian bread.

Serves 4

Stuffed artichokes

1/4 cup raw almonds
4 artichokes
3/4 cup ricotta cheese
2 garlic cloves, crushed
1 cup fresh bread crumbs
1 teaspoon finely grated lemon zest
1/2 cup grated Parmesan cheese
1/4 cup chopped Italian parsley
1 tablespoon olive oil
2 tablespoons butter
2 tablespoons lemon juice

Preheat the oven to 350°F. Spread the almonds on a baking tray and bake for 5–10 minutes or until lightly golden. Watch the almonds carefully, as they can burn easily. Cool, remove from the tray, and chop.

Remove any tough outer leaves from the artichokes. Cut across the artichokes, about 1 1/4 inches from the top, and trim the stalks, leaving about 3/4 inch. Rub the artichokes with lemon and put them in a bowl of cold water with a little lemon juice to prevent them from turning brown.

Combine the almonds, ricotta, garlic, bread crumbs, lemon zest, Parmesan, and parsley in a bowl and season with salt and pepper. Gently separate the artichoke leaves and push the filling in between the leaves. Place the artichokes carefully in a steamer and drizzle with the olive oil. Steam for 25–30 minutes or until tender (test with a metal skewer). Remove and place under a broiler for about 5 minutes to brown the filling.

Melt the butter in a saucepan, remove from the heat, and stir in the lemon juice. Arrange the artichokes on a serving plate, drizzle with the butter sauce, and season to taste.

Serves 4

Vegetable frittata with hummus and black olives

2 large red peppers
4 medium orange sweet potatoes
  (1 lb. 5 oz.), cut into ½-inch slices
¼ cup olive oil
2 leeks, finely sliced
2 garlic cloves, crushed
1 large zucchini (9 oz.), thinly sliced
2 large eggplants (1 lb. 2 oz.), cut
  into ½-inch slices
8 eggs, lightly beaten
2 tablespoons finely chopped basil
1¼ cups grated Parmesan cheese
1 cup store-bought hummus
black olives, pitted and halved,
  to garnish

Cut the peppers into large pieces, removing the seeds and membrane. Place, skin-side up, under a hot broiler until the skin blackens and blisters. Cool in a plastic bag. Peel.

Cook the sweet potatoes in a pot of boiling water for 4–5 minutes or until just tender. Drain.

Heat 1 tablespoon of the oil in a large frying pan and stir the leek and garlic over medium heat for 1 minute or until soft. Add the zucchini and cook for 2 minutes, then remove from the pan.

Heat the remaining oil in a large ovenproof pan and cook the eggplant in batches for 2 minutes on each side or until golden. Line the base of the pan with half the eggplant, then the leek. Cover with the pepper, the remaining eggplant, and the sweet potato.

Combine the eggs, basil, Parmesan, and some black pepper. Pour the mixture over the vegetables. Cook over low heat for 15 minutes or until almost cooked. Put the pan under a hot broiler for 2–3 minutes or until golden and cooked. Cool, then invert onto a cutting board. Cut into thirty squares. Top each square with some hummus and half an olive.

Makes 30 pieces

Caramelized onion tartlets with feta and thyme

1 1/2 sheets frozen piecrust
2 tablespoons unsalted butter
4 medium red onions (1 lb. 10 oz.),
  thinly sliced
1 1/2 tablespoons brown sugar
1 1/2 tablespoons balsamic vinegar
1 teaspoon chopped thyme
3 1/2 oz. feta cheese
thyme sprigs, to garnish

Preheat the oven to 350°F. Using a 2-inch round cutter, cut out twenty-four circles from the frozen piecrust. Place in lightly greased tartlet pans and bake for 15 minutes or until golden.

Meanwhile, melt the butter in a large frying pan. Add the red onion and cook over low heat for 35–40 minutes or until soft and golden. Add the brown sugar, balsamic vinegar, and thyme. Season with salt and pepper. Cook for another 10 minutes, then spoon into the tartlet shells.

Crumble the feta over the tartlets and place under a hot broiler for 30 seconds or until the cheese melts slightly. Top with sprigs of thyme and serve immediately.

Makes 24

Seasonal vegetable platter with saffron aioli

Saffron aioli
pinch of saffron threads
2 egg yolks
3 garlic cloves, crushed
2 tablespoons lemon juice
1 1/4 cups canola oil
white pepper, to taste

1 bunch baby carrots, scrubbed and trimmed, leaving 3/4 inch of green stem
1 bunch green asparagus, ends trimmed
1 cup baby corn
1 cup green beans, trimmed
2 Belgian endive, bases trimmed and leaves separated
1 1/2 cups radishes, trimmed and washed well
sea salt, to serve
crusty bread, to serve

To make the aioli, place the saffron in a small bowl with 1 tablespoon of water. Put the egg yolks in a food processor with the garlic and lemon juice and blend until smooth. With the motor running, start adding the canola oil, a few drops at a time, until an emulsion forms, then add the remainder in a slow, steady stream until thick and fully combined. Slowly add 2 tablespoons of warm water to thin slightly, then season well with salt and white pepper. Spoon into a small bowl and stir in the saffron water. Refrigerate until needed.

Blanch the carrots in boiling salted water for 3 minutes, then drain and rinse in cold water. (If you like them crunchy, serve them raw.) Blanch the asparagus in boiling salted water for 2 minutes or until tender. Drain and rinse in cold water. Blanch the baby corn in boiling salted water for 1 minute, then drain and rinse. Blanch the green beans for 30 seconds in boiling salted water, then drain and rinse.

Arrange all the vegetables on a serving platter with the saffron aioli. Serve with sea salt and crusty bread.

Serves 4–6

Fresh veggie rolls

Dipping sauce
¼ cup sweet chili sauce
1 tablespoon lime juice

3½ oz. dried rice vermicelli
½ green mango, julienned
1 small cucumber, seeded and
   julienned
½ avocado, julienned
4 scallions, thinly sliced
½ cup cilantro leaves
2 tablespoons chopped Vietnamese
   mint
1 tablespoon sweet chili sauce, extra
2 tablespoons lime juice
20 square (6-inch) rice-paper
   wrappers

To make the dipping sauce, mix together the chili sauce and lime juice.

Place the vermicelli in a bowl, cover with boiling water, and leave for 5 minutes or until softened. Drain, then cut into short lengths.

Put the vermicelli, mango, cucumber, avocado, scallions, coriander, mint, sweet chili sauce, and lime juice in a bowl and mix together well.

Working with no more than two rice-paper wrappers at a time, dip each wrapper in a bowl of warm water for 10 seconds to soften, then lay out on a flat work surface. Put 1 tablespoon of the filling on the wrapper, fold in the sides, and roll up tightly. Repeat with the remaining filling and wrappers. Serve immediately with the dipping sauce.

Makes 20

Note: Make sure the veggie rolls are tightly rolled together or they will fall apart while you are eating them.
   These rolls can be made 2–3 hours ahead of time—layer the rolls in an airtight container between sheets of waxed paper or plastic wrap and store in the refrigerator.

Asparagus gremolata

4 tablespoons butter
1 cup fresh white bread crumbs
¼ cup chopped Italian parsley
2 garlic cloves, very finely chopped
1 tablespoon very finely chopped
  lemon zest
14 oz. green asparagus, trimmed
1½ tablespoons virgin olive oil

Melt the butter in a heavy-based frying pan over high heat. Add the bread crumbs, and using a wooden spoon, stir until the crumbs are golden and crisp. Remove to a plate to cool slightly.

Combine the parsley, garlic, and lemon zest in a bowl, add the bread crumbs, and season to taste with freshly ground black pepper.

Bring a large saucepan of water to a boil, add the asparagus, and cook for 2–3 minutes or until just tender when pierced with a fine skewer. Drain well and arrange on a warmed serving plate. Drizzle with the olive oil and sprinkle the gremolata over the top. Serve immediately.

Serves 4

Mushroom pâté with melba toast

4 tablespoons butter
1 small onion, chopped
3 garlic cloves, crushed
4 cups button mushrooms, quartered
1 cup slivered almonds, toasted
2 tablespoons cream
2 tablespoons finely chopped
  thyme
3 tablespoons finely chopped
  Italian parsley
6 thick slices whole-wheat bread

Heat the butter in a large frying pan. Cook the onion and garlic over medium heat for 2 minutes or until soft. Increase the heat, add the mushrooms, and cook for 5 minutes or until the mushrooms are soft and most of the liquid has evaporated. Leave to cool for 10 minutes.

Put the almonds in a food processor or blender and chop roughly. Add the mushroom mixture and process until smooth. With the motor running, gradually pour in the cream. Stir in the herbs and season with salt and cracked black pepper. Spoon into two 1-cup ramekins and smooth the surface. Cover and refrigerate for 4–5 hours to allow the flavors to develop.

To make the toast, preheat the oven to 350°F. Toast one side of the bread under a hot broiler until golden. Remove the crusts and cut each slice into four triangles. Place on a baking sheet in a single layer, toasted-side down, and bake for 5–10 minutes or until crisp. Spread with pâté and serve immediately.

Makes 24

Vegetable shapes with crème fraîche and fried leeks

6 medium long, thin orange sweet
    potatoes (1 lb. 14 oz.)
5 beets
1/2 cup crème fraîche
1 garlic clove, crushed
1/4 teaspoon grated lime zest
vegetable oil, for deep-frying
2 leeks, cut lengthwise into very
    fine slices

Bring two large saucepans of water to a boil and place the sweet potatoes in one and the beets in the other. Boil, covered, for 30–40 minutes or until tender, adding more boiling water if it starts to evaporate. Drain separately and set aside until cool enough to touch. Remove the skins from the beets. Trim the ends from the beets and sweet potatoes and cut both into 1/2-inch slices. Using a cookie cutter, cut the slices into shapes. Leave to drain on paper towels.

Place the crème fraîche, garlic, and lime zest in a bowl and mix together well. Refrigerate until ready to use.

Fill a deep, heavy-based saucepan one-third full of oil and heat until a cube of bread dropped into the oil browns in 10 seconds. Cook the leeks in four batches for 30 seconds or until golden brown and crisp. Drain well on crumpled paper towels and season with salt.

To assemble, place a teaspoon of the crème fraîche mixture on top of each vegetable shape and top with some fried leek.

Makes 35

Red pepper and walnut dip with toasted pita wedges

4 large red peppers
1 small red chili
4 garlic cloves
1 cup walnuts, lightly toasted
3 slices sourdough bread, crusts
  removed
2 tablespoons lemon juice
1 tablespoon pomegranate
  molasses
1 teaspoon ground cumin
pita bread, to serve
olive oil, to drizzle
sea salt, to sprinkle

Cut the peppers into large, flat pieces. Place on a baking tray, skin-side up, with the chili and the whole garlic cloves, and cook under a hot broiler until the skin blackens and blisters. Transfer to a plastic bag and allow to cool. Gently peel away the pepper and chili skins and remove the garlic skins.

Place the walnuts in a food processor and grind. Add the pepper and chili flesh, garlic, bread, lemon juice, pomegranate molasses, and cumin and blend until smooth. Stir in 2 tablespoons of warm water to even out the texture, then season well with salt. Cover and refrigerate overnight so the flavors develop.

Preheat the oven to 400°F. Cut the pita bread into wedges, brush with olive oil, and lightly sprinkle with sea salt. Toast in the oven for 5 minutes or until golden brown. Allow to cool and become crisp.

Drizzle olive oil over the dip. Serve with the toasted pita wedges.

Serves 6–8

Indonesian peanut fritters

Dipping sauce
1 tablespoon rice vinegar
1 tablespoon mirin
2 tablespoons kecap manis
¼ teaspoon finely grated
   fresh ginger

1 cup rice flour
1 garlic clove, crushed
1 teaspoon ground turmeric
½ teaspoon ground cumin
1 tablespoon sambal oelek
1½ teaspoons ground coriander
1 tablespoon finely chopped cilantro
   leaves
scant 1 cup coconut milk
1¼ cups roasted unsalted peanuts
vegetable oil, for deep-frying

To make the dipping sauce, combine all the ingredients and cover.

To make the peanut fritters, combine the rice flour, garlic, turmeric, cumin, sambal oelek, coriander, cilantro leaves, and ½ teaspoon salt in a bowl. Gradually add the coconut milk until the mixture is smooth. Stir in the peanuts and ¼ cup hot water.

Fill a wok or deep, heavy-based saucepan one-third full of oil and heat until a cube of bread dropped into the oil browns in 15 seconds. Cook level tablespoons of the mixture in batches for 1–2 minutes or until golden. Drain on paper towels and season well with salt and pepper. Serve at once with the dipping sauce.

Makes 25

Roast squash, feta cheese, and pine nut pastries

1 lb. 12 oz. squash, skin removed,
    flesh cut into ½-inch-thick slices
2 tablespoons olive oil
3 garlic cloves, crushed
4 (6-inch) squares of puff pastry
3½ oz. marinated feta cheese
3 tablespoons oregano leaves,
    roughly chopped
2 tablespoons pine nuts, toasted
1 egg yolk
1 tablespoon milk
1 tablespoon sesame seeds
sea salt, to sprinkle

Preheat the oven to 425°F. Place the squash on a baking tray and toss with the olive oil, garlic, and salt and pepper. Roast in the oven for 40 minutes or until cooked and golden. Remove and allow to cool.

Evenly divide the squash among the four pastry squares, placing it in the center. Top with the feta, oregano, and pine nuts. Drizzle with a little of the feta marinating oil. Bring two opposite corners together and pinch in the center above the filling. Bring the other two opposite corners together and pinch to seal along the edges. The base will be square and the top will form a pyramid. Twist the top to seal where all four corners meet.

Place the egg yolk and milk in a small bowl and whisk with a fork.

Place the pastries on a greased baking sheet and brush with the egg and milk mixture. Sprinkle with sesame seeds and sea salt and bake for 15 minutes or until golden brown.

Serves 4

Vegetable dumplings

1 tablespoon vegetable oil
3 scallions, sliced
2 garlic cloves, chopped
2 teaspoons grated fresh ginger
3 tablespoons chopped garlic chives
2 lb. choy sum, shredded
2 tablespoons sweet chili sauce
3 tablespoons chopped cilantro
  leaves
¼ cup water chestnuts, drained
  and chopped
25 gow gee wrappers

Dipping sauce
½ teaspoon sesame oil
½ teaspoon peanut oil
1 tablespoon soy sauce
1 tablespoon lime juice
1 small red chili, finely chopped

Heat the oil in a frying pan over medium heat and cook the scallions, garlic, ginger, and garlic chives for 1–2 minutes or until soft. Increase the heat to high, add the choy sum, and cook for 4–5 minutes or until wilted. Stir in the chili sauce, cilantro, and water chestnuts. Allow to cool. If the mixture is too wet, squeeze dry.

Lay a gow gee wrapper on a flat work surface. Place a heaping teaspoon of the filling in the center. Moisten the edge of the wrapper with water and pinch to seal, forming a ball, then trim. Repeat with the remaining gow gee wrappers and filling.

Fill a wok halfway up its sides with water and bring to a boil. Line a bamboo steamer with baking parchment. Steam the dumplings, seam-side up, for 5–6 minutes.

To make the dipping sauce, combine all the ingredients. Serve with the dumplings.

Makes 25

Stuffed mushrooms

8 large porcini mushrooms
3 tablespoons butter
6 scallions, chopped
3 garlic cloves, crushed
2 cups day-old bread crumbs
1½ tablespoons finely chopped
  oregano
2 tablespoons chopped Italian parsley
½ cup grated Parmesan cheese
1 egg, lightly beaten
olive oil, for greasing and drizzling

Preheat the oven to 400°F. Remove the stems from the mushrooms and discard. Wipe the caps with a clean, damp cloth to remove any dirt.

Melt the butter in a small frying pan over medium heat, add the scallions, and cook for 2 minutes or until soft. Add the crushed garlic and cook for another minute. Place the bread crumbs in a bowl and add the scallion mixture, then the herbs, Parmesan, and beaten egg. Season with salt and freshly cracked black pepper and mix together well.

Lightly grease a baking tray. Divide the stuffing evenly among the mushrooms, pressing down lightly. Arrange the mushrooms on the tray, drizzle with olive oil, and bake in the oven for 15 minutes or until the tops are golden and the mushrooms are cooked through and tender. Serve immediately.

Serves 8

Mini spinach pies

⅓ cup olive oil
2 onions, finely chopped
2 garlic cloves, chopped
1½ cups small button mushrooms,
  roughly chopped
7 oz. spinach, chopped
½ teaspoon chopped thyme
3½ oz. feta cheese, crumbled
2 homemade or frozen piecrusts
milk, to glaze

Heat 2 tablespoons of oil in a frying pan over medium heat and cook the onion and garlic for 5 minutes or until soft and lightly browned. Add the mushrooms and cook for 4 minutes or until softened. Transfer to a bowl.

Heat 1 tablespoon of oil in the same pan over medium heat, add half the spinach, and cook, stirring well, for 2–3 minutes or until the spinach has softened. Add to the bowl with the onion. Repeat with the remaining oil and spinach. Add the thyme and feta to the bowl and mix. Season with salt and pepper and set aside to cool.

Preheat the oven to 400°F and grease two twelve-cup muffin pans. Flatten half the piecrust between two sheets of waxed paper and cut out twenty-four circles using a 2¾-inch cutter. Use these to line the muffin pans, then fill each muffin cup with some of the spinach mixture. Roll out the remaining piecrust between the waxed paper and cut out twenty-four more circles, again using a 2¾-inch cutter. Cover the pies with the lids and press the edges with a fork to seal. Prick the tops once with a fork, brush with milk, and bake for 15–20 minutes or until golden.

Makes 24

Eggplant, tomato, and goat cheese stack

4 vine-ripened tomatoes
4 garlic cloves, chopped
1 tablespoon shredded basil
2 tablespoons finely chopped
   Italian parsley
1/4 cup olive oil
1 large eggplant (9 oz.), cut into
   1/4-inch slices
8 basil leaves, extra, torn
3 oz. goat cheese, crumbled

Preheat the oven to 350°F. Halve the tomatoes and scoop out the pulp. Sprinkle a quarter of the garlic into each tomato half, then top with the combined basil and parsley. Arrange the halves on a baking tray, drizzle with 1 tablespoon of oil, season to taste, and bake for 40 minutes or until soft.

Preheat the broiler. Brush a baking tray with olive oil, place the eggplant slices on the tray, and brush with the remaining oil. Broil for 5 minutes or until crisp and golden.

Lightly oil four 3/4-cup ramekins. Line each with a slice of eggplant, then two basil leaves, a piece of tomato, some goat cheese, another piece of tomato, and top with a final slice of eggplant. Bake for 20 minutes, then leave for 5 minutes before turning out.

Serves 4

Cauliflower fritters

1 small head cauliflower (1 lb. 5 oz.)
1/2 cup besan (chickpea flour)
2 teaspoons ground cumin
1 teaspoon ground coriander
1 teaspoon ground turmeric
pinch of cayenne pepper
1 egg, lightly beaten
1 egg yolk, extra
vegetable oil, for deep-frying

Cut the cauliflower into bite-size florets. Sift the flour and spices into a bowl, then stir in 1/2 teaspoon salt.

Lightly whisk the beaten egg, egg yolk, and 1/4 cup water in a bowl. Make a well in the center of the dry ingredients and pour in the egg mixture, whisking until smooth. Let stand for 30 minutes.

Fill a deep saucepan one-third full of oil and heat to 350°F or until a cube of bread dropped into the oil browns in 15 seconds. Dip the florets into the batter, allowing the excess to drain into the bowl. Deep-fry in batches for 3–4 minutes per batch or until puffed and browned. Drain, sprinkle with salt and extra cayenne, if desired, and serve hot.

Serves 4–6

Mini Thai spring rolls

Filling
3 oz. dried rice vermicelli
2 garlic cloves, crushed
1 carrot, grated
4 scallions, finely chopped
1 tablespoon sweet chili sauce
2 teaspoons grated fresh ginger
2 cilantro roots, finely chopped
1½ tablespoons lime juice
1 teaspoon brown sugar
2 tablespoons chopped cilantro
   leaves
1 tablespoon sesame oil
1 tablespoon kecap manis

40 (5-inch) square spring roll
   wrappers
vegetable oil, for deep-frying
sweet chili sauce, to serve

To make the filling, soak the vermicelli in boiling water for 5 minutes. Drain and cut into short lengths. Mix with the remaining filling ingredients.

Working with one wrapper at a time, spoon 1 tablespoon of the filling onto one corner, brush the edges with water, and roll up diagonally, tucking in the edges as you go. Repeat with the remaining filling and wrappers.

Fill a wok or deep, heavy-based saucepan one-third full of oil and heat until a cube of bread browns in 15 seconds. Cook in batches for 2–3 minutes or until golden brown. Drain on paper towels. Serve with sweet chili sauce.

Makes 40

Baked stuffed peppers

2 red peppers
2 yellow peppers
2 teaspoons olive oil
16 basil leaves
2½ tablespoons capers in vinegar,
    drained, rinsed, and chopped
3 tablespoons olive oil, extra
2 garlic cloves, crushed
1 tablespoon balsamic vinegar

Preheat the oven to 350°F. Cut the peppers in half lengthwise, leaving the stems intact (if they are very large, cut them into quarters). Scrape out the seeds and any excess pith. Drizzle the bottom of an ovenproof dish with the 2 teaspoons of olive oil and add the peppers, skin-side down.

Place two basil leaves in each pepper, then divide the chopped capers among them. Season well with salt and freshly ground pepper.

In a bowl, combine the extra olive oil with the garlic and balsamic vinegar, then drizzle evenly over the peppers. Cover the dish with foil and cook for 10–15 minutes or until the peppers are partially cooked.

Remove the foil and cook for another 15–20 minutes or until the peppers are tender and golden on the edges. Serve warm or at room temperature.

Serves 4

Betel and tofu bites

2 tablespoons sugar
24 betel leaves or large basil leaves
1 tablespoon vegetable oil
2 garlic cloves, crushed
1 tablespoon grated fresh ginger
2 small red chilies, seeded and finely
    chopped
7 oz. fried tofu puffs, shredded
2 fresh kaffir lime leaves, finely
    shredded
3 tablespoons lime juice
2 tablespoons brown sugar
3 tablespoons cilantro leaves
1/4 cup dried coconut, toasted

In a bowl, combine the sugar and
2 cups water. Stir in the betel leaves,
soak for 10 minutes, then drain.

Heat the oil in a frying pan and
cook the garlic, ginger, and chili
over medium heat for 1 minute.
Add the tofu, lime leaves, and the
combined lime juice, brown sugar,
and coriander. Stir until the tofu is
heated through.

Put 1 tablespoon of the tofu mixture
onto each betel leaf and lightly
sprinkle with coconut. Roll up the
leaves tightly and serve.

Makes 24

Beet hummus

1 lb. 2 oz. beets (about 10 medium)
⅓ cup olive oil
1 large onion, chopped
1 tablespoon ground cumin
14-oz. can chickpeas, drained
1 tablespoon tahini
⅓ cup plain yogurt
3 garlic cloves, crushed
¼ cup lemon juice
½ cup vegetable stock
Lebanese or Turkish bread, to serve

Scrub the beets well. Bring a large saucepan of water to a boil over high heat and cook the beets for 35–40 minutes or until soft and cooked through. Drain and cool slightly before peeling.

Meanwhile, heat 1 tablespoon of the oil in a frying pan over medium heat and cook the onion for 2–3 minutes or until soft. Add the cumin and cook for another 1 minute or until fragrant.

Chop the beets and place in a food processor or blender with the onion mixture, chickpeas, tahini, yogurt, garlic, lemon juice, and stock and process until smooth. With the motor running, add the remaining oil in a thin, steady stream. Process until the mixture is thoroughly combined. Serve the hummus with Lebanese or Turkish bread.

Serves 8

Note: You can use 1 lb. 2 oz. of any vegetable to make the hummus. Try carrots or squash.

Stuffed zucchini flowers

½ cup all-purpose flour
3½ oz. mozzarella cheese
10 basil leaves, torn
20 zucchini flowers, stems and
  pistils removed
olive oil, for shallow-frying
2 lemon wedges, to serve

In a bowl, combine the flour with about 1 cup water, or enough to obtain a creamy consistency. Add a pinch of salt and mix.

Cut the mozzarella cheese into twenty matchsticks. Insert a piece of mozzarella and some basil into each zucchini flower. Gently press the petals closed.

Pour oil into a heavy-based frying pan to a depth of 1 inch. Heat until a drop of batter sizzles when dropped in the oil.

Dip one flower at a time in the batter, shaking off the excess. Cook in batches for 3 minutes or until crisp and golden. Drain on paper towels. Season and serve immediately with lemon wedges.

Makes 20

Vegetable pakoras with spiced yogurt

Spiced yogurt
1 teaspoon cumin seeds
scant 1 cup plain yogurt
1 garlic clove, crushed
1/2 cup cilantro leaves, chopped

1/3 cup besan (chickpea flour)
1/3 cup self-rising flour
1/3 cup soy flour
1/2 teaspoon ground turmeric
1 teaspoon cayenne pepper
1/2 teaspoon ground coriander
1 small green chili, seeded and
    finely chopped
vegetable oil, for deep-frying
1/2 head cauliflower (7 oz.), cut into
    small florets
1 medium orange sweet potato
    (5 oz.), cut into 1/4-inch slices
1 medium eggplant (6 oz.), cut into
    1/4-inch slices
6 oz. fresh asparagus, cut into
    2 1/2-inch lengths

To make the spiced yogurt, heat a small frying pan over medium heat. Add the cumin seeds and dry-fry for 1–2 minutes or until aromatic (shake the pan frequently to prevent the seeds from burning). Transfer to a mortar and pestle or spice grinder and roughly grind. Whisk into the yogurt with the garlic. Season with salt and freshly ground black pepper, then stir in the cilantro leaves.

Place the besan, self-rising and soy flours, turmeric, cayenne, ground coriander, chili, and 1 teaspoon salt in a bowl. Gradually whisk in 1 cup cold water to form a batter. Leave for 15 minutes. Preheat the oven to 250°F.

Fill a small saucepan one-third full of oil and heat until a cube of bread browns in 20 seconds. Dip the vegetables in the batter and deep-fry in small batches for 1–2 minutes or until pale golden. Remove with a slotted spoon and drain well on paper towels. Keep warm in the oven until all the vegetables are cooked.

Serve the hot vegetable pakoras with the spiced yogurt.

Serves 4

Individual Italian summer tarts

1/4 cup olive oil
2 red onions, sliced
1 tablespoon balsamic vinegar
1 teaspoon brown sugar
1 tablespoon chopped thyme
1 sheet rolled puff pastry
6-oz. jar marinated quartered
  artichokes, drained
16 black olives, pitted
extra-virgin olive oil, to serve
thyme sprigs, to garnish

Heat 2 tablespoons of the olive oil in a saucepan over low heat. Add the onion and cook, stirring occasionally, for 15 minutes or until soft. Add the vinegar and brown sugar and cook for 15 minutes or until lightly browned. Remove from the heat, stir in the chopped thyme, and set aside to cool.

Preheat the oven to 425°F and heat a lightly greased baking sheet. Cut four 4-inch rounds from the sheet of puff pastry and spread the onion over them, leaving a 1/2-inch border.

Place the pastry bases on the hot baking sheet and cook in the top half of the oven for 12–15 minutes or until the edges are risen and the pastry is golden brown.

Arrange the artichokes over the onion, then fill the spaces with olives. Drizzle the tarts with extra-virgin olive oil and serve garnished with thyme.

Serves 4

Artichokes in aromatic vinaigrette

2 tablespoons lemon juice
4 large artichokes
2 garlic cloves, crushed
1 teaspoon finely chopped oregano
$\frac{1}{2}$ teaspoon ground cumin
$\frac{1}{2}$ teaspoon ground coriander
pinch of dried chili flakes
1 tablespoon sherry vinegar
$\frac{1}{4}$ cup olive oil

Add the lemon juice to a large bowl of cold water. Trim the artichokes, cutting off the stalks to within 2 inches of the base and removing the tough outer leaves. Cut the top quarter of the leaves from each artichoke. Slice each artichoke in half from the top to the base, or into quarters if large. Remove each small, furry heart with a teaspoon, then put the artichokes in the bowl of lemon water to prevent them from discoloring while you prepare the rest.

Bring a large, nonreactive saucepan of water to a boil, add the artichokes and a teaspoon of salt, and simmer for 20 minutes or until tender. The cooking time will depend on the size of the artichokes. Test by pressing a skewer into the base. If cooked, the artichoke will be soft and give little resistance. Strain, then place the artichokes on their cut side to drain.

Combine the garlic, oregano, cumin, coriander, and chili flakes in a bowl. Season to taste and blend in the vinegar. Beating constantly, slowly pour in the oil to form an emulsion. This can be done in a food processor.

Arrange the artichokes in rows on a platter. Pour the vinaigrette over the top and leave to cool completely.

Serves 4

Spinach and leek fritters

3 tablespoons butter
1/4 cup pine nuts
1 leek, white part only, thinly sliced
3 1/2 oz. baby spinach, chopped
3 eggs
1 egg yolk
1 tablespoon cream
3/4 cup grated Parmesan cheese
1 tablespoon chopped parsley
1 tablespoon olive oil

Melt half the butter in a heavy-based frying pan over low–medium heat and cook the pine nuts and leek for 3 minutes or until the pine nuts are golden. Add the spinach and cook for 1 minute. Remove the mixture from the pan and allow to cool slightly. Wipe out the pan with paper towels.

Whisk the eggs, yolk, and cream together in a large bowl. Add the cheese and parsley and season with salt and freshly ground black pepper. Stir in the spinach mixture.

Melt half of the remaining butter and half of the olive oil in the frying pan. Place four 2 1/2-inch egg rings in the pan and pour 1/4 cup of the spinach mixture into each ring. Cook over low heat for 2–3 minutes or until the base is set. Gently flip and cook the other side for 2–3 minutes or until firm. Transfer to a plate and slide out of the egg rings. Repeat with the remaining butter, oil, and spinach mixture. Serve immediately.

Makes 8

Potato tortilla

3 medium potatoes (1 lb. 2 oz.),
  cut into ½-inch slices
¼ cup olive oil
1 brown onion, thinly sliced
4 garlic cloves, thinly sliced
2 tablespoons finely chopped
  Italian parsley
6 eggs

Place the potato slices in a large
saucepan, cover with cold water, and
bring to a boil. Boil for 5 minutes, then
drain and set aside.

Heat the oil in a deep-sided, nonstick
frying pan over medium heat. Add
the onion and garlic and cook for
5 minutes or until the onion softens.

Add the potato and parsley to the
pan and stir to combine. Cook over
medium heat for 5 minutes, gently
pressing down into the pan.

Whisk the eggs with 1 teaspoon
each of salt and freshly ground black
pepper and pour the eggs evenly
over the potatoes. Cover and cook
over low–medium heat for about
20 minutes or until the eggs are just
set. Slide onto a serving plate or
serve directly from the pan.

Serves 6–8

Udon noodle sushi rolls

10½ oz. flat udon or soba noodles
6 sheets roasted nori
1¾ oz. pickled daikon, cut into
  long, thin strips
3 tablespoons drained red pickled
  ginger shreds
ponzu sauce, for dipping (see Note)

Cook the udon or soba noodles according to the instructions on the package or until tender. Rinse under cold water and pat dry.

Working on a flat surface, lay one sheet of nori on a sushi mat. Top with one-sixth of the noodles along the bottom half of the nori, then arrange the daikon and the pickled ginger along the center of the noodles. Roll the nori up firmly to enclose the filling. Cut the roll in half and then each half into three equal pieces. Repeat with the remaining ingredients. Serve with the ponzu sauce.

Makes 36 pieces

Note: Ponzu is a Japanese dipping sauce made from rice vinegar, soy, mirin, and dashi.

Individual vegetable terrines with spicy tomato sauce

½ cup vegetable oil
2 zucchini, sliced diagonally
2 large eggplants (1 lb. 2 oz.), sliced
1 small fennel bulb, sliced
1 red onion, sliced
1¼ cups ricotta cheese
½ cup grated Parmesan cheese
1 tablespoon chopped Italian parsley
1 tablespoon chopped chives
1 red and 1 yellow pepper, broiled,
  peeled, and cut into large pieces

Spicy tomato sauce
1 tablespoon vegetable oil
1 onion, finely chopped
2 garlic cloves, crushed
1 red chili, seeded and chopped
15-oz. can chopped tomatoes
2 tablespoons tomato paste

Heat 1 tablespoon of the oil in a large frying pan over high heat. Cook the zucchini, eggplant, fennel, and onion in batches for 5 minutes or until golden, adding more oil as needed. Drain separately on paper towels.

Preheat the oven to 400°F. Mix together the ricotta, Parmesan, parsley, and chives. Season well.

Lightly grease and line four 1¼-cup ramekins. Using half the eggplant, line the base of each ramekin. Continue layering with the zucchini, peppers, cheese mixture, fennel, and onion. Cover with the remaining eggplant and press down firmly. Bake for 10–15 minutes or until hot. Leave for 5 minutes before turning out.

Meanwhile, to make the sauce, heat the oil in a saucepan and cook the onion and garlic for 2–3 minutes or until soft. Add the chili, chopped tomatoes, and tomato paste and simmer for 5 minutes or until thick and pulpy. Puree in a food processor. Return to the saucepan and keep warm. Spoon over the terrines.

Serves 4

Soups

Jerusalem artichoke and roast garlic soup

1 garlic head
2 tablespoons butter
1 tablespoon olive oil
1 onion, chopped
1 leek, white part only, washed
  and chopped
1 celery stalk, chopped
1 lb. 9 oz. Jerusalem artichokes,
  peeled and chopped
1 small potato, chopped
6 cups vegetable or chicken stock
olive oil, to serve
finely chopped chives, to serve

Preheat the oven to 400°F. Slice the base from the head of garlic, wrap it in foil, and roast for 30 minutes or until soft. When cool enough to handle, remove from the foil and slip the cloves from the skin. Set aside.

In a large, heavy-based saucepan, heat the butter and oil. Add the onion, leek, and celery and a large pinch of salt and cook for 10 minutes or until soft. Add the Jerusalem artichokes, potato, and garlic and cook for another 10 minutes. Pour in the stock, bring the mixture to a boil, then reduce the heat and simmer for 30 minutes or until the vegetables are soft.

Puree in a blender until smooth, then season well with salt and pepper. Serve with a drizzle of olive oil and some chives. Delicious with warm crusty bread.

Serves 4

Miso soup with udon and tofu

1 teaspoon dashi granules
3 tablespoons red (genmai) miso
   paste
2 tablespoons soy sauce
14 oz. fresh udon noodles, separated
14 oz. silken firm tofu, cubed
1 cup fresh shiitake mushrooms,
   sliced
1 bunch baby bok choy, leaves
   separated

Place the dashi, miso, soy sauce, and 5 cups water in a large saucepan and bring to a boil. Reduce the heat and simmer for 10 minutes.

Add the udon noodles and cook for 5 minutes or until soft. Stir in the tofu, shiitake mushrooms, and bok choy and cook for 3 minutes or until the bok choy wilts. Serve immediately.

Serves 2–4

Green soup with pistou

¼ cup olive oil
1 onion, finely chopped
2 garlic cloves, crushed
1 celery stalk, chopped
1 zucchini, cut into ½-inch rounds
1 head broccoli, cut into ½-inch
  pieces
6 cups vegetable or chicken stock
1 cup green beans, trimmed, cut into
  ½-inch pieces
1 cup green peas
1 bunch asparagus, ends trimmed,
  cut into ½-inch pieces
2 cups shredded Swiss chard leaves

Pistou
3 garlic cloves, peeled
⅔ cup basil
⅓ cup olive oil
½ cup grated Parmesan cheese

Heat the olive oil in a large saucepan and cook the onion, garlic, and celery until golden. Add the zucchini and broccoli and cook for 5 minutes.

Add the stock and bring to a boil. Simmer for 5 minutes, then add the green beans, peas, asparagus, and Swiss chard. Simmer for 5 minutes or until the vegetables are tender. Season well with salt and pepper.

To make the pistou, place the garlic and basil in a mortar and pestle or food processor and crush together. Slowly add the oil and blend until it becomes a smooth paste. Stir in the Parmesan and season well with salt and pepper.

Ladle the soup into bowls and serve with a dollop of pistou.

Serves 4

Borscht

6 large beets (3 lb. 5 oz.), peeled
1½ tablespoons superfine sugar
½ cup lemon juice
3 eggs
sour cream, to serve (optional)

Grate the beets and place in a saucepan with the sugar and 9 cups water. Stir over low heat until the sugar has dissolved. Simmer, partially covered, for about 30 minutes, skimming the surface occasionally.

Add the lemon juice and simmer, uncovered, for 10 minutes. Remove the pan from the heat.

Whisk the eggs in a bowl. Gradually pour the eggs into the beet mixture, whisking constantly and being careful not to curdle the eggs. Season to taste with salt and pepper. Allow the soup to cool, then cover and refrigerate until cold. Delicious served with a dollop of sour cream.

Serves 6

Gazpacho

6 medium vine-ripened tomatoes
(2 lb. 4 oz.), chopped
1 cucumber, chopped
1 small red pepper, seeded and
chopped
1 red onion, chopped
3 garlic cloves
3 slices sourdough bread, crusts
removed
2 tablespoons sherry vinegar
hot pepper sauce

Dressing
2 teaspoons each of finely diced
tomato, red pepper, red onion,
and cucumber
2 teaspoons finely chopped
Italian parsley
1 tablespoon extra-virgin olive oil
1 teaspoon lemon juice

In a blender, place the tomatoes,
cucumber, red pepper, onion, garlic,
sourdough bread, and 1 cup cold
water and blend until smooth. Pass
through a strainer into a bowl, then
add the sherry vinegar. Season to
taste with salt and hot pepper sauce,
then cover and refrigerate for at least
2 hours or overnight to allow the
flavors to develop.

To make the dressing, combine all the
ingredients in a small bowl. Season to
taste with salt and pepper.

Stir the gazpacho well, then ladle into
bowls. Spoon the dressing on top
before serving.

Serves 4

Vegetable soup

1/2 cup dried red kidney beans or
  borlotti beans
1 tablespoon olive oil
1 leek, halved lengthwise and
  chopped
1 small onion, diced
2 carrots, chopped
2 celery stalks, chopped
1 large zucchini, chopped
1 tablespoon tomato paste
4 cups vegetable stock
14 oz. butternut squash, cut into
  3/4-inch cubes
2 potatoes, cut into 3/4-inch cubes
3 tablespoons chopped Italian parsley

Place the beans in a large bowl, cover
with cold water, and soak overnight.
Rinse, then transfer to a saucepan,
cover with cold water, and cook for
45 minutes or until just tender. Drain.

Heat the olive oil in a saucepan. Add
the leek and onion and cook over
medium heat for 2–3 minutes, without
browning, until they start to soften.
Add the carrot, celery, and zucchini
and cook for 3–4 minutes. Add the
tomato paste and stir for 1 minute.
Pour in the vegetable stock and
5 cups water and bring to a boil.
Reduce the heat to low and simmer
for 20 minutes.

Add the squash, potato, parsley,
and beans and simmer for another
20 minutes or until the vegetables
are tender and the beans are cooked.
Season well. Serve with crusty bread.

Serves 6

Laksa

7 oz. dried rice vermicelli
2 tablespoons peanut oil
2–3 tablespoons laksa paste
4 cups vegetable stock
3 cups coconut milk
1½ cups snow peas, halved
   diagonally
5 scallions, cut into 1¼-inch lengths
2 tablespoons lime juice
1 cup bean sprouts
1 cup fried tofu puffs, halved
3 tablespoons roughly chopped
   Vietnamese mint
⅔ cup cilantro leaves

Place the vermicelli in a large bowl, cover with boiling water, and soak for 5 minutes.

Heat the oil in a large saucepan, add the laksa paste, and cook, stirring, over medium heat for 1 minute or until fragrant. Add the stock, coconut milk, snow peas, and scallions and simmer for 5 minutes. Pour in the lime juice and season to taste with salt and freshly ground black pepper.

Drain the vermicelli and divide among four bowls. Top with the bean sprouts and fried tofu puffs. Ladle the hot soup into the bowls and sprinkle with the fresh mint and cilantro. Serve immediately.

Serves 4

Asparagus soup

1 lb. 10 oz. fresh asparagus spears
4 cups vegetable or chicken stock
1 tablespoon butter
1 tablespoon all-purpose flour
$1/2$ teaspoon finely grated lemon zest
extra lemon zest, to garnish

Trim and discard any woody ends from the asparagus spears and cut into $3/4$-inch lengths. Place in a large saucepan and add 2 cups of the stock. Cover and bring to a boil, then cook for 10 minutes or until the asparagus is tender.

Transfer the asparagus and the hot stock to a blender or food processor and puree in batches until smooth. Melt the butter in the saucepan over low heat, add the flour, then cook, stirring, for about 1 minute or until pale and foaming. Remove from the heat and gradually add the remaining stock, stirring until smooth after each addition. When all the stock has been added, return the saucepan to the heat, bring to a boil, then simmer for 2 minutes.

Add the asparagus puree to the pan and stir until combined. When heated through, stir in the lemon zest and season with salt and cracked black pepper. Garnish with the lemon zest.

Serves 4

Chili, corn, and red pepper soup

1 cilantro sprig
4 ears sweet corn
1 tablespoon butter
2 red peppers, diced
1 small onion, finely chopped
1 small red chili, finely chopped
1 tablespoon all-purpose flour
2 cups vegetable stock
1/2 cup cream

Trim the leaves off the cilantro and finely chop the root and stems. Cut the kernels off the ears of corn.

Heat the butter in a saucepan over medium heat. Add the corn kernels, red peppers, onion, and chili and stir to coat in the butter. Cook, covered, over low heat, stirring occasionally, for 10 minutes or until soft. Increase the heat to medium, add the cilantro root and stem, and cook, stirring, for 30 seconds or until fragrant. Sprinkle in the flour and stir for 1 minute. Remove from the heat and gradually stir in the stock. Add 2 cups water and return to the heat. Bring to a boil, reduce the heat to low, and simmer, covered, for 30 minutes or until the vegetables are tender. Cool slightly.

Ladle 2 cups of the soup into a blender and puree until smooth. Return the puree to the soup in the pan, pour in the cream, and gently heat until warmed through. Season with salt and pepper. Sprinkle with the cilantro leaves and serve. Delicious with grilled cheese on pita bread.

Serves 4

Soba noodle and vegetable soup

9 oz. soba noodles
2 dried shiitake mushrooms
8 cups vegetable stock
1/2 cup snow peas, cut into strips
2 small carrots, cut into thin 2-inch
  strips
2 garlic cloves, finely chopped
6 scallions, cut into 2-inch lengths
  and thinly sliced lengthwise
1 1/4-inch piece ginger, julienned
1/3 cup soy sauce
1/4 cup mirin or sake
1 cup bean sprouts
cilantro leaves, to garnish

Cook the noodles according to the instructions on the package. Drain.

Soak the mushrooms in 1/2 cup boiling water until soft. Drain, reserving the liquid. Remove the stalks and slice the mushrooms.

Combine the stock, mushrooms, reserved liquid, snow peas, carrots, garlic, scallions, and ginger in a large saucepan. Bring slowly to a boil, then reduce the heat to low and simmer for 5 minutes or until the vegetables are tender. Add the soy sauce, mirin, and bean sprouts. Cook for another 3 minutes.

Divide the noodles among four large serving bowls. Ladle the hot liquid and vegetables on top and garnish with cilantro.

Serves 4

Squash and red lentil soup

1 tablespoon olive oil
1 long red chili, seeded and chopped
1 onion, finely chopped
1 lb. 2 oz. butternut squash, chopped
2 medium orange sweet potatoes
   (12 oz.), chopped
6 cups vegetable stock
½ cup red lentils
1 tablespoon tahini
red chili, extra, to garnish

Heat the oil in a large saucepan over medium heat, add the chili and onion, and cook for 2–3 minutes or until the onion is soft. Reduce the heat to low, add the squash and sweet potatoes, and cook, covered, for 8 minutes, stirring occasionally.

Increase the heat to high, add the stock, and bring to a boil. Reduce the heat to low and simmer, covered, for 10 minutes. Add the red lentils and cook, covered, for 7 minutes or until tender.

Process the soup in batches in a blender or food processor, add the tahini, and blend until smooth. Return to the saucepan and gently heat until warmed through. Garnish with chili.

Serves 4

Carrot and ginger soup

3 cups vegetable stock
1 tablespoon vegetable oil
1 onion, chopped
1 tablespoon grated fresh ginger
8 medium carrots (2 lb. 4 oz.),
    chopped
2 tablespoons chopped cilantro

Place the stock in a pan and bring to a boil. Heat the oil in a large, heavy-based pan, add the onion and ginger, and cook for 2 minutes or until the onion has softened.

Add the stock and carrots. Bring to a boil, then reduce the heat and simmer for 10–15 minutes or until the carrots are cooked and tender.

Place in a blender or food processor and process in batches until smooth. Return to the pan and add a little more stock or water to thin the soup to your desired consistency.

Stir in the cilantro and season to taste with salt and pepper. Heat gently before serving.

Serves 4

Thai spicy sour soup

3 cups vegetable stock
2 tablespoons Tom Yum paste
  (see Note)
3/4 x 3/4-inch piece galangal, peeled
  and cut into thin slices
1 stem lemongrass, lightly crushed
  and cut into 4 lengths
3 fresh kaffir lime leaves
1 small red chili, finely sliced
  diagonally (optional)
2 cups button mushrooms, halved
1 cup silken firm tofu, cut into
  1/2-inch cubes
7 oz. baby bok choy, roughly
  shredded
2 tablespoons lime juice
4 tablespoons cilantro leaves

Place the stock, Tom Yum paste, galangal, lemongrass, kaffir lime leaves, chili, and 3 cups water in a saucepan. Cover and bring to a boil, then reduce the heat and simmer for 5 minutes.

Add the mushrooms and tofu and simmer for 5 minutes or until the mushrooms are tender. Add the bok choy and simmer for another minute or until wilted. Remove the pan from the heat and stir in the lime juice and cilantro leaves before serving.

Serves 4–6

Note: For vegetarian cooking, make sure you buy a brand of Tom Yum paste that does not contain shrimp paste or fish sauce.

Swiss chard and risoni soup with Gruyère croutons

1 tablespoon butter
1 large onion, finely chopped
1 garlic clove, crushed
8 cups vegetable or chicken stock
1 cup risoni (rice-shaped pasta)
½ baguette, cut into 6 slices
1 teaspoon butter, extra, melted
1 teaspoon Dijon mustard
1¾ oz. Gruyère cheese, coarsely grated
1 lb. 2 oz. Swiss chard, central stalk removed, shredded
1 cup basil, torn

Heat the butter in a large, heavy-based saucepan, add the onion and garlic, and cook over medium heat for 2–3 minutes or until the onion is softened. Meanwhile, place the stock in a separate pan and bring to a boil.

Add the stock to the onion mixture and bring to a boil. Add the risoni, reduce the heat, and simmer for 8 minutes, stirring occasionally.

Meanwhile, place the baguette slices in a single layer on a baking sheet and cook under a preheated broiler until golden brown on one side. Turn the slices over and brush with the combined melted butter and mustard. Top with the Gruyère and grill until the cheese has melted.

Add the Swiss chard and basil to the risoni mixture and simmer for about 1 minute or until the risoni is al dente and the Swiss chard is cooked. Season with salt and freshly ground black pepper and serve with the Gruyère croutons.

Serves 6

Potato and sweet corn chowder

6 ears sweet corn
2 tablespoons vegetable oil
1 onion, finely diced
3 garlic cloves, crushed
1 celery stalk, diced
1 carrot, peeled and diced
2 large potatoes, peeled and diced
4 cups vegetable or chicken stock
2 tablespoons finely chopped
  Italian parsley

Bring a large pot of salted water to a boil and cook the sweet corn for 5 minutes. Reserve 1 cup of the cooking water. Cut the corn kernels from the ears, place half in a blender with the reserved cooking water, and blend until smooth.

Heat the oil in a large saucepan, add the onion, garlic, celery, and a large pinch of salt, and cook for 5 minutes. Add the carrot and potatoes, cook for another 5 minutes, then add the stock, corn kernels, and blended corn mixture. Reduce the heat and simmer for 20 minutes or until the vegetables are tender. Season well and stir in the chopped parsley before serving.

Serves 6

Curried lentil, carrot, and cashew soup

6 cups vegetable or chicken stock
6 medium carrots (1 lb. 10 oz.),
    grated
3/4 cup red lentils, rinsed and
    drained
1 tablespoon olive oil
1 large onion, chopped
1/2 cup unsalted cashew nuts
1 tablespoon Madras curry paste
1/2 cup chopped cilantro leaves
    and stems
1/2 cup plain yogurt
cilantro leaves, extra, to garnish

Bring the stock to a boil in a large saucepan. Add the carrots and lentils, bring the mixture back to a boil, then simmer over low heat for about 8 minutes or until the carrots and lentils are soft.

Meanwhile, heat the oil in a pan, add the onion and cashews, and cook over medium heat for 2–3 minutes or until the onion is soft and browned. Add the curry paste and cilantro leaves and cook for another minute or until fragrant. Stir the paste into the carrot and lentil mixture.

Transfer to a food processor or blender and process in batches until smooth. Return the mixture to the pan and reheat over medium heat until hot. Season to taste with salt and cracked black pepper and serve with a dollop of yogurt and a sprinkling of cilantro.

Serves 6

Note: Garnish the soup with a pinch of chili flakes to give it an extra kick.

Spicy parsnip soup

5 cups vegetable or chicken stock
1 tablespoon butter
1 white onion, cut into quarters
  and finely sliced
1 leek, finely sliced
1 lb. 2 oz. parsnips, peeled and
  finely sliced
1 tablespoon Madras curry powder
1 teaspoon ground cumin
1 1/4 cups cream
1/3 cup cilantro leaves

Bring the stock to a boil in a saucepan and keep at a low simmer.

Place the butter in a large saucepan and melt over medium heat. Add the onion, leek, and parsnip and cook, covered, for 5 minutes. Add the curry powder and cumin and cook for 1 minute. Stir in the stock and cook, covered, over medium heat for about 10 minutes or until tender.

Transfer the soup to a blender or food processor and blend in batches until smooth. Return to the pan. Stir in the cream and warm through over low heat. Season to taste with salt and cracked black pepper and sprinkle with cilantro leaves.

Serves 6

Note: This soup is also delicious without the cream.

Tomato and pasta soup

5 cups vegetable or chicken stock
1 cup spiral pasta
2 carrots, sliced
1 zucchini, sliced
4 ripe tomatoes, roughly chopped
2 tablespoons shredded basil
fresh whole-grain bread, to serve

Place the stock in a heavy-based saucepan and bring to a boil. Reduce the heat, add the pasta, carrots, and zucchini, and cook for 5–10 minutes or until the pasta is al dente.

Add the tomato and heat through gently for a few more minutes. Season to taste.

Pour the soup into warm soup bowls and sprinkle the basil over the top. Serve with fresh whole-grain bread.

Serves 4

Variation: To give this soup a slightly different flavor, serve with a dollop of fresh pesto.

Green curry vegetable soup

2 teaspoons peanut oil
1 tablespoon green curry paste
3 kaffir lime leaves
5 cups vegetable or chicken stock
2²/₃ cups coconut milk
1 lb. 5 oz. butternut squash, cut into
   ¹/₂-inch cubes
9 oz. small yellow squash, sliced
4 oz. fresh baby corn, halved
   lengthwise
2 tablespoons mushroom soy sauce
2 tablespoons lime juice
1 teaspoon sugar
1¹/₂ tablespoons Vietnamese mint,
   finely chopped

Heat the oil in a large saucepan and add the curry paste and lime leaves. Cook, stirring, over medium heat for 1 minute or until the mixture is fragrant. Bring the stock to a boil in a separate saucepan.

Gradually add the stock and coconut milk to the curry mixture and bring to a boil. Add the squash and corn and simmer over low heat for 12 minutes or until the squash is tender.

Add the soy sauce and lime juice and season to taste with sugar, salt, and black pepper. Sprinkle with the mint before serving.

Serves 6

Sweet potato
and pear soup

1 tablespoon butter
1 small white onion, finely chopped
5 medium orange sweet potatoes
   (1 lb. 10 oz.), peeled and cut into
   3/4-inch dice
2 firm pears (1 lb. 2 oz.), peeled,
   cored, and cut into 3/4-inch dice
3 cups vegetable or chicken stock
1 cup cream
mint leaves, to garnish

Melt the butter in a saucepan over medium heat, add the onion, and cook for 2–3 minutes or until softened but not brown. Add the sweet potatoes and pears and cook, stirring, for 1–2 minutes. Add the stock to the pan, bring to a boil, and cook for 20 minutes or until the sweet potatoes and pears are soft.

Cool slightly, then place the mixture in a blender or food processor and blend in batches until smooth. Return to the pan, stir in the cream, and gently reheat without boiling. Season with salt and ground black pepper. Garnish with the mint.

Serves 4

Mushroom and tortellini soup

1 tablespoon olive oil
1½ cups small flat mushrooms, sliced
6 scallions, sliced
1 small garlic clove, crushed
5 cups vegetable or chicken stock
1 tablespoon port
2 teaspoons Worcestershire sauce
7 oz. fresh, large ricotta tortellini
shaved Parmesan cheese, to garnish

Heat the oil in a large, heavy-based saucepan. Add the mushrooms and cook over high heat for 2 minutes, browning the mushrooms before turning. Add the scallions and garlic and cook for another minute.

Meanwhile, bring the stock to a boil in a separate saucepan. Add the stock, port, and Worcestershire sauce to the mushroom mixture and bring to a boil. Add the tortellini and simmer for 8 minutes or until the tortellini is al dente.

Season the soup with salt and cracked black pepper and serve topped with shaved Parmesan.

Serves 4

Spring vegetable soup with basil pesto

5 cups vegetable or chicken stock
1 tablespoon extra-virgin olive oil
8 scallions, finely sliced
2 celery stalks, finely sliced
12 baby carrots, sliced
2 bunches asparagus, woody ends
  removed, cut into 1¼-inch lengths
5½ oz. baby corn, cut into 1¼-inch
  lengths
¼ cup fresh or bottled pesto
extra-virgin olive oil, to thin pesto
  (see Note)
shaved Parmesan cheese, to garnish

Bring the stock to a boil in a large saucepan. Meanwhile, heat the olive oil in a large, heavy-based saucepan and add the scallions and celery. Cover and cook over medium heat for 5 minutes or until softened.

Add the stock to the scallion mixture and mix well.

Add the carrots, asparagus, and corn to the pan. Return the mixture to a boil, then reduce the heat and simmer for 10 minutes.

Spoon into warmed soup bowls. Top with a dollop of pesto, season to taste with salt and pepper, and garnish with shaved Parmesan.

Serves 4

Note: Homemade pesto or fresh pesto from a deli will provide a better flavor than bottled pesto. If you prefer a thinner pesto, mix it with a little olive oil to give it a runnier consistency.

Chilled garlic and almond soup

1 loaf day-old Italian bread, crust removed
1 cup whole blanched almonds
3–4 garlic cloves, chopped
1/2 cup extra-virgin olive oil
1/3 cup sherry or white-wine vinegar
1 1/4–1 1/2 cups vegetable stock
2 tablespoons olive oil, extra
2 slices day-old Italian bread, extra, crust removed, cut into 1/2-inch cubes
1 cup small seedless green grapes

Soak the bread in cold water for 5 minutes, then squeeze out any excess liquid. Chop the almonds and garlic in a processor until well ground. Add the bread and process until the mixture is smooth.

With the motor running, add the olive oil in a steady, slow stream until the mixture is the consistency of thick mayonnaise. Slowly add the sherry and 1 1/4 cups of the stock. Blend for 1 minute. Season to taste with salt. Refrigerate for at least 2 hours. The soup thickens in the refrigerator, so you may need to add extra stock or water to thin it.

When ready to serve, heat the extra oil in a frying pan, add the bread cubes, and toss over medium heat for 2–3 minutes or until golden. Drain on crumpled paper towels. Serve the soup very cold, garnished with the grapes and bread cubes.

Serves 4–6

Spinach soup

1 tablespoon butter
1 onion, finely chopped
3 medium floury (e.g., russet)
   potatoes (1 lb. 2 oz.), grated
4 cups vegetable or chicken stock
1 lb. 2 oz. frozen chopped spinach
1/4 teaspoon ground nutmeg
sour cream, to serve

Melt the butter in a large saucepan, add the chopped onion, and cook, stirring occasionally, until soft but not browned.

Add the grated potatoes and stock to the pan and mix well, scraping the onion from the bottom of the pan. Add the frozen spinach and cook, covered, until the spinach has thawed and broken up, stirring occasionally. Uncover and simmer for 10–15 minutes or until the potatoes are very soft. Stir the soup frequently while it cooks to keep it from sticking on the bottom. Transfer to a blender or food processor and blend in batches until smooth.

Return the soup to the pan and gently reheat. Add the nutmeg and season with salt and black pepper. Ladle into bowls, add a dollop of sour cream to each bowl, and swirl into the soup.

Serves 4

Zuppa di faggioli

2 (14-oz.) cans cannellini beans
1 tablespoon extra-virgin olive oil
1 leek, finely chopped
2 garlic cloves, crushed
1 teaspoon thyme leaves
2 celery stalks, diced
1 carrot, diced
2 lb. 4 oz. Swiss chard, trimmed and
　roughly chopped
1 ripe tomato, diced
4 cups vegetable stock
2 small crusty rolls, each cut into
　4 slices
2 teaspoons balsamic vinegar
⅓ cup finely grated Parmesan cheese

Put one can of beans and its liquid in a blender or small food processor and blend until smooth. Drain the other can, reserving the beans and discarding the liquid.

Heat the oil in a large, heavy-based saucepan, add the leek, garlic, and thyme, and cook for 2–3 minutes or until soft and aromatic. Add the celery, carrot, Swiss chard, and tomato and cook for 2–3 minutes or until the Swiss chard has wilted. Heat the stock in a separate saucepan.

Stir the pureed cannellini beans and stock into the vegetable mixture. Bring to a boil, then reduce the heat and simmer for 5–10 minutes or until the vegetables are tender. Add the drained beans and stir until heated through. Season to taste with salt and cracked black pepper.

Arrange two slices of bread in the base of each soup bowl. Stir the balsamic vinegar into the soup and ladle over the bread. Serve topped with grated Parmesan.

Serves 4

Note: This recipe is an authentic bean soup from Florence. If you like, spice it up by adding some chopped chili.

Split pea and vegetable soup

1 tablespoon peanut or
  vegetable oil
1 onion, chopped
2 garlic cloves, chopped
1 1/2 teaspoons chopped fresh
  ginger
1 1/2 tablespoons Madras curry
  paste
1/2 cup yellow split peas, rinsed
  and drained
1 large zucchini, peeled and chopped
1 large carrot, roughly chopped
1 3/4 cups button mushrooms, roughly
  chopped
1 celery stalk, roughly chopped
4 cups vegetable stock
1/2 cup cream

Heat the oil in a saucepan, add the onion, and cook over low heat for 5 minutes or until soft. Add the garlic, ginger, and curry paste and cook over medium heat for 2 minutes. Stir in the split peas until well coated with paste, then add the zucchini, carrot, mushrooms, and celery and cook for 2 minutes.

Add the stock, bring to a boil, then reduce the heat and simmer, partly covered, for 1 hour. Remove from the heat and allow to cool slightly.

Transfer the soup to a blender or food processor and process in batches until smooth. Return to the pan, stir in the cream, and gently heat until warmed through. Delicious served with naan bread.

Serves 4

Red pepper, spinach, and chickpea soup

1 tablespoon olive oil
8 scallions, finely sliced
1 red pepper
1 garlic clove, crushed
1 teaspoon cumin seeds
1 1/2 cups Italian tomato sauce
3 cups vegetable or beef stock
10 1/2-oz. can chickpeas, rinsed
  and drained
2 teaspoons red-wine vinegar
1–2 teaspoons sugar
3 1/2 oz. baby spinach leaves

Heat the oil in a large, heavy-based saucepan and stir in the scallions. Reduce the heat and cook, covered, for 2–3 minutes or until softened. Meanwhile, remove the seeds and membrane from the red pepper and dice finely. Add the red pepper, garlic, and cumin seeds to the pan and cook for 1 minute.

Add the tomato sauce and stock and bring the mixture to a boil. Reduce the heat and simmer for 10 minutes. Add the chickpeas, vinegar, and sugar to the soup and simmer for another 5 minutes.

Stir in the baby spinach and season to taste with salt and ground black pepper. Cook until the spinach begins to wilt, then serve immediately.

Serves 4

Cream of fennel and leek soup

1 tablespoon butter
2 large fennel bulbs, thinly sliced
2 leeks, thinly sliced
4 cups hot vegetable or chicken stock
2 rosemary sprigs
1/8 teaspoon ground nutmeg
1/3 cup sour cream
1/4 cup finely grated Parmesan cheese
1 tablespoon vegetable oil
1 leek, extra, cut in half lengthwise,
  then cut into 1 1/2-inch lengths
grated Parmesan cheese, extra,
  to garnish
sour cream, extra, to garnish

Heat the butter in a large, heavy-based saucepan, add the sliced fennel and leek, and cook, covered, over medium heat for 2–3 minutes, stirring occasionally.

Put the hot stock, rosemary sprigs, and nutmeg in a saucepan and bring to a boil. Simmer over low heat for about 15 minutes, then remove the rosemary sprigs and add the fennel and leek mixture to the pan.

Transfer the soup to a blender or food processor and blend in batches until smooth. Return to the pan and stir in the sour cream and Parmesan. Reheat over medium heat until hot. Season to taste with salt and cracked black pepper and keep warm.

Heat the oil in a frying pan and cook the extra leek for 2–3 minutes or until soft but not browned.

Spoon the soup into six warm soup bowls and top with the fried leek. Garnish with the extra Parmesan and sour cream and serve immediately.

Serves 6

Fresh mushroom, shallot, and sour cream soup

2 tablespoons butter
4 French shallots, roughly chopped
3 garlic cloves, crushed
1 cup firmly packed Italian parsley
1 1/4 cups vegetable or chicken stock
1 1/4 cups milk
5 cups button mushrooms
1/4 teaspoon ground nutmeg
1/4 teaspoon cayenne pepper
2/3 cup light sour cream
cayenne pepper, to garnish

Melt the butter in a large, heavy-based saucepan and add the shallots, garlic, and parsley. Cook over medium heat for 2–3 minutes. Put the stock and milk in a separate saucepan and bring to a boil.

Gently wipe the mushrooms, then chop and add to the shallot mixture. Season with salt and pepper and stir in the nutmeg and cayenne pepper. Cook, stirring, for 1 minute. Add the stock and milk, bring to a boil, then reduce the heat and simmer for 5 minutes. Transfer the soup to a blender or food processor and blend until smooth. Return to the pan.

Stir in the sour cream, adjust the seasoning, and reheat gently. Serve sprinkled with cayenne pepper.

Serves 4

Note: For an ideal garnish, fry diced button mushrooms in a little butter until golden. They can be prepared just before the soup is done.

Asian noodle soup

8 dried Chinese mushrooms
3½ oz. dried rice vermicelli
1 lb. 12 oz. Chinese broccoli, cut into
  2-inch lengths
8 fried tofu puffs, cut into strips
1 cup bean sprouts
4 cups vegetable stock
2 tablespoons light soy sauce
1½ tablespoons Chinese rice wine
3 scallions, finely chopped
cilantro leaves, to serve

Place the dried mushrooms in a bowl, cover with boiling water, and soak for 15 minutes. Drain, reserving ½ cup of the liquid. Squeeze the mushrooms to remove any excess liquid. Discard the stems and thinly slice the caps.

Soak the vermicelli in boiling water for 5 minutes. Drain. Divide the vermicelli, broccoli, tofu puffs, and bean sprouts among four serving bowls.

Place the reserved mushroom liquid, stock, soy sauce, rice wine, scallions, and mushrooms in a saucepan and bring to a boil. Cook, covered, for 10 minutes.

Ladle the soup into the serving bowls and garnish with the cilantro leaves.

Serves 4

Vegetable and lentil soup with spiced yogurt

2 tablespoons olive oil
1 small leek, white part only, chopped
2 garlic cloves, crushed
2 teaspoons curry powder
1 teaspoon ground cumin
1 teaspoon garam masala
4 cups vegetable stock
1 bay leaf
1 cup brown lentils
1 lb. butternut squash, peeled and cut into 1/2-inch cubes
2 zucchini, cut in half lengthwise and sliced
14-oz. can chopped tomatoes
7 oz. broccoli, cut into small florets
1 small carrot, diced
1/2 cup peas
1 tablespoon chopped mint

Spiced yogurt
1 cup thick plain yogurt
1 tablespoon chopped cilantro leaves
1 garlic clove, crushed
3 dashes hot pepper sauce

Heat the oil in a saucepan over medium heat. Add the leek and garlic and cook for 4–5 minutes or until soft and lightly golden. Add the curry powder, cumin, and garam masala and cook for 1 minute or until fragrant.

Add the stock, bay leaf, lentils, and squash. Bring to a boil, then reduce the heat to low and simmer for 10–15 minutes or until the lentils are tender. Season well.

Add the zucchini, tomatoes, broccoli, carrot, and 2 cups water and simmer for 10 minutes or until the vegetables are tender. Add the peas and simmer for 2–3 minutes.

To make the spiced yogurt, place the yogurt, cilantro, garlic, and hot pepper sauce in a small bowl and stir until combined.

Dollop a spoonful of the yogurt on each serving of soup and garnish with the chopped mint.

Serves 6

Squash soup

2 cups vegetable stock
1 lb. 10 oz. butternut squash, cut into
 1/2-inch cubes
2 onions, chopped
2 garlic cloves, halved
1/4 teaspoon ground nutmeg
1/4 cup cream
crusty bread, to serve

Put the stock and 2 cups water in a large, heavy-based saucepan and bring to a boil. Add the squash, onions, and garlic and return to a boil. Reduce the heat slightly and cook for 15 minutes or until the squash is soft.

Drain the vegetables through a colander, reserving the liquid. Puree the squash mixture in a blender until smooth (you may need to add some of the reserved liquid). Return the squash puree to the pan and stir in enough of the reserved liquid to reach the desired consistency. Season to taste with nutmeg, salt, and cracked black pepper.

Ladle the soup into four soup bowls and pour some cream into each bowl to create a swirling pattern on the top. Serve with warm, crusty bread.

Serves 4

Potato and arugula soup

6 cups vegetable or chicken stock
2 lb. 12 oz. red potatoes, chopped
  into small pieces
2 large garlic cloves, peeled, left
  whole
9 oz. arugula
1 tablespoon extra-virgin olive oil
extra arugula leaves, to garnish
  (optional)
½ cup shaved Parmesan cheese

Place the stock in a large, heavy-based saucepan and bring to a boil. Add the potatoes and garlic and simmer over medium heat for 15 minutes or until the potatoes are tender. Add the arugula and simmer for another 2 minutes. Stir in the olive oil.

Transfer the mixture to a blender or food processor and blend in batches until smooth. Return the mixture to the pan and stir over medium heat until hot. Season to taste with salt and cracked black pepper and serve in warmed bowls. Garnish with the extra arugula leaves and shaved Parmesan before serving.

Serves 6

Broth with ravioli

3 cups vegetable or chicken stock
9 oz. spinach and ricotta ravioli
1/2 cup snow peas, sliced diagonally
2 tablespoons chopped Italian parsley
2 tablespoons chopped basil
grated Parmesan cheese, to garnish

Place the stock in a large, heavy-based saucepan and bring to a boil. Add the ravioli and cook for 8–10 minutes or until the pasta is al dente.

Season to taste with salt and pepper and stir in the snow peas, parsley, and basil. Pour the soup into two bowls and sprinkle with grated Parmesan before serving.

Serves 2

Spicy roast-pepper soup

4 red peppers
2 teaspoons vegetable oil
2 garlic cloves, crushed
4 scallions, sliced
1 teaspoon finely chopped seeded chilies
15-oz. can crushed tomatoes
1/2 cup chilled vegetable stock
1 teaspoon balsamic vinegar
2 tablespoons chopped basil

Cut the peppers into quarters and remove the seeds and membrane. Place the peppers skin-side up under a hot broiler and broil until the skins blacken and blister. Cool in a plastic bag, then peel away the skin and roughly chop the flesh.

Heat the oil in a small saucepan, add the garlic, scallions, and chili, and cook over low heat for 1–2 minutes or until softened.

Transfer to a food processor or blender and add the peppers, crushed tomatoes, and stock. Blend until smooth, then stir in the vinegar and basil. Season to taste with salt and cracked pepper. Refrigerate, then serve cold.

Serves 4

Sweet potato and chili soup

1 tablespoon vegetable oil
1 onion, chopped
2 garlic cloves, finely chopped
1–2 small red chilies, finely chopped
1/4 teaspoon paprika
5 medium orange sweet potatoes
   (1 lb. 10 oz.), chopped into small
   pieces
4 cups vegetable or beef stock
chopped dried chili, to garnish

Heat the oil in a large, heavy-based saucepan, add the onion, and cook for 1–2 minutes or until soft. Add the garlic, chili, and paprika and cook for another 2 minutes or until aromatic. Add the sweet potatoes to the pan and toss to coat with the spices.

Pour in the stock, bring to a boil, then reduce the heat and simmer for 15 minutes or until the vegetables are tender. Cool slightly, then transfer to a blender or food processor and blend in batches until smooth, adding extra water if needed to reach the desired consistency. Do not overblend or the mixture may become gluey.

Season to taste with salt and black pepper. Ladle the soup into bowls, sprinkle with dried chili, and serve.

Serves 4

Zucchini pesto soup

1 tablespoon olive oil
1 large onion, finely chopped
2 garlic cloves, crushed
3 cups vegetable or chicken stock
6 medium zucchini (1 lb. 10 oz.),
   thinly sliced
¼ cup cream
toasted ciabatta bread, to serve

Pesto
1 cup basil
¼ cup finely grated Parmesan cheese
2 tablespoons pine nuts, toasted
2 tablespoons extra-virgin olive oil

Heat the oil in a large, heavy-based saucepan. Add the onion and garlic and cook over medium heat for 5 minutes or until the onion is soft.

Bring the stock to a boil in a separate saucepan. Add the zucchini and hot stock to the onion mixture. Bring to a boil, then reduce the heat, cover, and simmer for about 10 minutes or until the zucchini is very soft.

To make the pesto, process the basil, Parmesan, and pine nuts in a food processor for 20 seconds or until finely chopped. Gradually add the olive oil and process until smooth. Spoon into a small bowl.

Transfer the zucchini mixture to a blender or food processor and blend in batches until smooth. Return the mixture to the pan, stir in the cream and 2 tablespoons of the pesto, and reheat over medium heat until hot. Season with salt and black pepper and serve with toasted ciabatta bread. Serve the remaining pesto in a bowl for diners to help themselves, or cover with olive oil and store in the refrigerator for up to 1 week.

Serves 4

Minestrone

½ cup macaroni
1 tablespoon olive oil
1 leek, sliced
2 garlic cloves, crushed
1 carrot, sliced
1 waxy potato (e.g., red or pink eye),
  chopped
1 zucchini, sliced
2 celery stalks, sliced
1 cup green beans, cut into short
  lengths
15-oz. can chopped tomatoes
8 cups vegetable or beef stock
2 tablespoons tomato paste
15-oz. can cannellini beans, rinsed
  and drained
2 tablespoons chopped Italian parsley
shaved Parmesan cheese, to serve

Bring a saucepan of water to a boil, add the macaroni, and cook for 10–12 minutes or until al dente. Drain.

Meanwhile, heat the oil in a large, heavy-based saucepan, add the leek and garlic, and cook over medium heat for 3–4 minutes.

Add the carrot, potato, zucchini, celery, green beans, tomatoes, stock, and tomato paste. Bring to a boil, then reduce the heat and simmer for 10 minutes or until the vegetables are tender.

Stir in the cooked pasta and cannellini beans and heat through. Spoon into warmed serving bowls and garnish with parsley and shaved Parmesan.

Serves 4

Note: Just about any vegetable can be added to minestrone, so this is a great recipe for using up leftover vegetables.

Chickpea, potato, and spinach soup

4 cups vegetable stock
1 1/2 tablespoons olive oil
1 onion, finely chopped
1 large potato, cut into 1/2-inch cubes
1 1/2 teaspoons paprika
2 garlic cloves, crushed
14-oz. can chickpeas, drained
1 large tomato, cut into small
  cubes
1 cup spinach, coarsely shredded
1/4 cup grated Parmesan cheese

Place the stock in a saucepan, then cover and slowly bring to a boil. Heat the olive oil in a large, heavy-based saucepan and cook the onion for 2–3 minutes or until soft.

Add the potato to the onion and stir in the paprika, garlic, and chickpeas. Add the onion mixture to the stock and bring to a boil. Stir in the tomato and season with salt and cracked black pepper.

Simmer for 10 minutes or until the potato is tender. Add the spinach and cook until wilted. Top with Parmesan, season to taste, and serve.

Serves 4

Saffron and Jerusalem artichoke soup

pinch of saffron threads
9 oz. Jerusalem artichokes
2 tablespoons lemon juice
1 tablespoon olive oil
1 large onion, finely chopped
4 cups vegetable or chicken stock
1 tablespoon ground cumin
3 medium red potatoes (1 lb. 2 oz.), grated
2 teaspoons lemon juice, extra

Place the saffron threads in a bowl with 2 tablespoons boiling water and leave until needed. Peel and thinly slice the artichokes, dropping the slices into a bowl of water mixed with lemon juice to prevent discoloration.

Heat the oil in a large, heavy-based saucepan, add the onion, and cook over medium heat for 2–3 minutes or until the onion is softened. Bring the stock to a boil in a separate saucepan. Add the cumin to the onion mixture and cook for another 30 seconds or until fragrant. Add the drained artichokes, potatoes, saffron mixture, stock, and extra lemon juice. Bring to a boil, then reduce the heat and simmer for 15–18 minutes or until the artichokes are very soft.

Transfer to a blender and process in batches until smooth. Return the soup to the pan and season to taste with salt and cracked pepper. Reheat over medium heat and serve.

Serves 4

Salads

Moroccan carrot salad with green olives and mint

1 1/2 teaspoons cumin seeds
1/2 teaspoon coriander seeds
1 tablespoon red-wine vinegar
2 tablespoons olive oil
1 garlic clove, crushed
2 teaspoons harissa
1/4 teaspoon orange flower water
1 lb. 5 oz. baby carrots, tops
   trimmed, well scrubbed
1/3 cup large green olives, pitted and
   finely sliced
2 tablespoons shredded mint
1 cup watercress leaves

In a small frying pan, dry-fry the cumin and coriander seeds for 30 seconds or until fragrant. Cool and then grind in a mortar and pestle or spice grinder. Place in a large mixing bowl with the red-wine vinegar, olive oil, garlic, harissa, and orange flower water. Whisk to combine.

Blanch the carrots in boiling salted water for 5 minutes, until almost tender. Drain into a colander and allow to sit for a few minutes until they dry. While still hot, add to the red-wine vinegar dressing and toss gently to coat. Allow to cool to room temperature so the dressing can infuse into the carrots. Add the green olives and mint. Season with salt and pepper and toss gently to combine. Serve on the watercress leaves.

Serves 4

Roasted beet salad

2 tablespoons red-wine vinegar
1/3 cup walnut oil
1 garlic clove, crushed
1 teaspoon Dijon mustard
12 shallots
12 garlic cloves
6 medium beets, scrubbed well
1 tablespoon vegetable oil
2 cups baby beet leaves
1/2 cup walnuts, toasted

Preheat the oven to 400°F. In a small bowl, whisk together the red-wine vinegar, walnut oil, garlic, and Dijon mustard. Season well with sea salt and pepper. Set aside.

Roast the shallots, garlic, and beets for 1 hour. Remove from the oven and continue to roast the beets for another 30 minutes or until tender when pierced with a skewer.

Slip the shallots and garlic from their skin and cut the beets into wedges. Add the dressing to the vegetables, toss together, and let cool to room temperature.

In a large bowl, place the beet leaves, walnuts, and vegetables with the dressing, season well with sea salt and pepper, and gently toss together. Arrange on a serving platter or individual plates.

Serves 4

Grilled cauliflower salad with sesame dressing

Sesame dressing
3 tablespoons tahini
1 garlic clove, crushed
¼ cup seasoned rice-wine vinegar
1 tablespoon vegetable oil
1 teaspoon lime juice
¼ teaspoon sesame oil

1 medium head cauliflower
12 garlic cloves, crushed
2 tablespoons vegetable oil
2 heads romaine lettuce, washed
  well and drained
2 cups watercress leaves, washed
  well and drained
2 teaspoons sesame seeds, toasted
1 tablespoon finely chopped parsley

Preheat a grilling pan to medium heat. In a medium nonmetallic bowl, place the tahini, garlic, rice-wine vinegar, vegetable oil, lime juice, sesame oil, and 1 tablespoon water. Whisk together thoroughly until well combined and season to taste with salt and pepper.

Cut the cauliflower in half, then into ½-inch wedges. Place on a tray and gently rub with the garlic and vegetable oil. Season well. Grill the cauliflower pieces until golden on both sides and cooked through. Remove from the grilling pan.

Arrange the romaine leaves and watercress on a serving platter and top with the grilled cauliflower slices. Drizzle the dressing on top and garnish with the sesame seeds and parsley. Serve immediately.

Serves 4

Thai green papaya salad

1 lb. 2 oz. green papayas, peeled
   and seeded
1–2 small red chilies, thinly sliced
1 tablespoon brown sugar
1 tablespoon soy sauce
2 tablespoons lime juice
1 tablespoon fried garlic (see Note)
1 tablespoon fried shallots (see Note)
1/2 cup green beans, cut into 1/2-inch
   lengths
8 cherry tomatoes, quartered
2 tablespoons chopped roasted
   unsalted peanuts

Grate the papayas into long, fine
shreds with a zester or knife.

Place the papayas in a large mortar
and pestle with the chili, brown
sugar, soy sauce, and lime juice.
Lightly pound until combined. Add
the fried garlic and shallots, beans,
and tomatoes. Lightly pound for
another minute or until combined.
Serve immediately, sprinkled with
the peanuts.

Serves 4

Note: Packets of fried garlic and
shallots are available from Asian
markets.

Warm casareccia and sweet potato salad

5 medium orange sweet potatoes
   (1 lb. 10 oz.)
2 tablespoons extra-virgin olive oil
1 lb. 2 oz. casareccia or other short,
   thin pasta
11½ oz. marinated feta cheese in oil
3 tablespoons balsamic vinegar
1 bunch asparagus, cut into short
   lengths
3 cups arugula or spinach leaves
2 vine-ripened tomatoes, chopped
¼ cup pine nuts, toasted

Preheat the oven to 400°F. Peel the sweet potatoes and cut into large pieces. Place in a baking dish, drizzle with the olive oil, and season well with salt and cracked black pepper. Bake for 20 minutes or until the sweet potatoes are tender.

Cook the pasta in a large saucepan of boiling water until al dente. Drain well.

Drain the oil from the feta and whisk 3 tablespoons of the oil together with the balsamic vinegar to make a dressing.

Steam the asparagus until bright green and tender. Drain well.

Combine the pasta, sweet potatoes, asparagus, arugula, feta, tomatoes, and pine nuts in a bowl. Add the dressing and toss gently. Season with black pepper and serve immediately.

Serves 4

Insalata caprese

3 large vine-ripened tomatoes
9 oz. bocconcini cheese
12 basil leaves
¼ cup extra-virgin olive oil
4 basil leaves, roughly torn, extra

Slice the tomatoes into twelve ½-inch slices. Slice the bocconcini into twenty-four slices the same thickness as the tomato slices.

Arrange the tomato slices on a plate, alternating them with two slices of bocconcini and placing a basil leaf between the bocconcini slices.

Drizzle with the olive oil, sprinkle with the torn basil, and season well with salt and freshly ground black pepper.

Serves 4

Note: You could also use whole cherry tomatoes and toss them with the bocconcini and basil.

Warm potato salad with green olive dressing

3 lb. 5 oz. nicola potatoes (or any
small, waxy potato), scrubbed
½ cup green olives, pitted and finely
chopped
2 teaspoons capers, finely chopped
¾ cup parsley, finely chopped
2 tablespoons lemon juice
1 teaspoon finely grated lemon zest
2 garlic cloves, crushed
½ cup extra-virgin olive oil

Boil the potatoes for 15 minutes or
until just tender (pierce with the tip
of a sharp knife—if the potato flakes
easily, it is ready). Drain and allow to
cool slightly.

While the potatoes are cooking, place
the olives and capers in a small bowl
with the parsley, lemon juice, lemon
zest, garlic, and olive oil. Whisk with
a fork to combine.

Cut the potatoes into halves and
gently toss with the dressing while
still warm. Taste before seasoning
with fresh black pepper and a little
salt, if desired.

Serves 6

Gado gado

2 small carrots, thinly sliced
3½ oz. cauliflower, cut into small
    florets
1 cup snow peas, trimmed
1 cup bean sprouts
8 well-shaped iceberg lettuce leaves
4 small potatoes, cooked and cut into
    thin slices
1 cucumber, thinly sliced
2 hard-boiled eggs, peeled and cut
    into quarters
2 ripe tomatoes, cut into wedges

Peanut sauce
1 tablespoon vegetable oil
1 small onion, finely chopped
½ cup crunchy peanut butter
¾ cup coconut milk
1 teaspoon sambal oelek
1 tablespoon lemon juice
1 tablespoon kecap manis

Steam the carrots and cauliflower in a saucepan for 5 minutes or until nearly tender. Add the snow peas and cook for 2 minutes. Add the bean sprouts and cook for another minute. Remove from the heat and cool.

To make the peanut sauce, heat the oil in a saucepan and cook the onion for 5 minutes over low heat or until soft and lightly golden. Add the peanut butter, coconut milk, sambal oelek, lemon juice, kecap manis, and ¼ cup water and stir well. Bring to a boil, stirring constantly, then reduce the heat and simmer for 5 minutes or until the sauce has reduced and thickened. Remove from the heat.

Place two lettuce leaves together, one inside the other, to make four lettuce cups.

In each lettuce cup, arrange a quarter of the potatoes, carrots, cauliflower, snow peas, bean sprouts, and cucumber. Top with some of the peanut sauce and garnish with the eggs and tomatoes.

Serves 4

Roasted fennel and orange salad

8 baby fennel bulbs
5 tablespoons olive oil
2 oranges
1 tablespoon lemon juice
1 red onion, halved and thinly sliced
1/2 cup kalamata olives
2 tablespoons roughly chopped mint
1 tablespoon roughly chopped Italian
  parsley

Preheat the oven to 400°F. Trim the fronds from the fennel and reserve. Remove the stalks and cut a 1/4-inch slice off the base of each fennel. Slice each fennel into six wedges, put in a baking dish, and drizzle with 3 tablespoons olive oil. Season well with salt and pepper. Bake for 40–45 minutes or until tender and slightly caramelized. Turn once or twice during cooking. Allow to cool.

Cut a thin slice off the top and bottom of each orange. Using a sharp knife, slice off the skin and pith. Remove as much pith as possible. Slice down the side of a segment between the flesh and the membrane. Repeat with the other side and lift the segment out. Do this over a bowl to catch the juices. Repeat with all the segments on both oranges. Squeeze out any juice remaining in the membranes.

Whisk the remaining oil into the orange juice and lemon juice until emulsified. Season well. Combine the orange segments, onion, and olives in a bowl and add half the dressing and half the mint. Mix well. Transfer to a serving dish. Top with the fennel, drizzle with the remaining dressing, and sprinkle with the parsley and remaining mint. Chop up the reserved fronds and sprinkle on top.

Serves 4

Tabbouleh

¾ cup bulgur
3 ripe tomatoes
1 cucumber
4 scallions, sliced
4 cups chopped Italian parsley
½ cup chopped mint

Dressing
⅓ cup lemon juice
¼ cup olive oil
1 tablespoon extra-virgin olive oil

Place the bulgur in a bowl, cover with 2 cups water, and leave for 1½ hours.

Cut the tomatoes in half, squeeze to remove any excess seeds, and cut into ½-inch cubes. Cut the cucumber in half lengthwise, remove the seeds with a spoon, and cut the flesh into ½-inch cubes.

To make the dressing, place the lemon juice and 1½ teaspoons salt in a bowl and whisk until well combined. Season well with freshly ground black pepper and slowly whisk in the olive oil and extra-virgin olive oil.

Drain the bulgur and squeeze out any excess water. Spread the bulgur out on a clean dish towel or paper towels and leave to dry for about 30 minutes. Put the bulgur in a large salad bowl, add the tomatoes, cucumber, scallions, parsley, and mint, and toss well to combine.

Pour the dressing over the salad and toss until evenly coated.

Serves 6

Cucumber, feta, mint, and dill salad

4 oz. feta cheese
4 cucumbers
1 small red onion, thinly sliced
1 1/2 tablespoons finely chopped dill
1 tablespoon dried mint
3 tablespoons olive oil
1 1/2 tablespoons lemon juice

Crumble the feta into 1/2-inch pieces and place in a large bowl. Peel and seed the cucumbers and cut into 1/2-inch dice. Add to the bowl along with the onion and dill.

Grind the mint in a mortar and pestle, or force through a sieve, until powdered. Combine with the oil and juice, then season with salt and black pepper. Pour over the salad and toss well.

Serves 4

Warm choy sum salad

13 oz. choy sum
2 tablespoons peanut oil
1 tablespoon finely grated ginger
2 garlic cloves, finely chopped
2 teaspoons sugar
2 teaspoons sesame oil
2 tablespoons soy sauce
1 tablespoon lemon juice
2 teaspoons sesame seeds, toasted

Trim the ends from the choy sum and slice in half. Steam for 2 minutes or until wilted and arrange on a serving plate.

Heat a small saucepan until very hot, add the peanut oil, and swirl it around to coat the pan. Add the ginger and garlic and stir-fry for 1 minute. Add the sugar, sesame oil, soy sauce, and lemon juice, heat until hot, and pour over the choy sum. Season to taste, garnish with sesame seeds, and serve immediately.

Serves 4

Tomato salad with white beans

3 tablespoons olive oil
2 red shallots, finely diced
1 large garlic clove, crushed
1½ tablespoons lemon juice
9 oz. red cherry tomatoes, halved
9 oz. yellow pear tomatoes, halved
15-oz. can white beans, drained
  and rinsed
⅓ cup basil leaves, torn
2 tablespoons chopped parsley

Place the olive oil, diced shallots, crushed garlic, and lemon juice in a small bowl and whisk to combine.

Place the halved cherry and pear tomatoes and the white beans in a serving bowl. Drizzle with the dressing and sprinkle the basil and parsley on top. Toss gently to combine.

Serves 4

Beet and chive salad

3 lb. 5 oz. baby beets, unpeeled,
  trimmed and washed
1/2 cup walnut halves
2 cups roughly chopped watercress
1 1/2 tablespoons snipped chives
  (3/4-inch lengths)

Dressing
1/4 teaspoon honey
1/4 teaspoon Dijon mustard
1 tablespoon balsamic vinegar
2 tablespoons olive oil

Preheat the oven to 400°F. Place the beets in a roasting pan, cover with foil, and roast for 1 hour or until tender when pierced with a skewer. Remove from the oven and peel when cool enough to handle.

Meanwhile, for the dressing, combine the honey, mustard, and balsamic vinegar in a small pitcher. Whisk in the oil with a fork until well combined and season to taste with salt and freshly ground black pepper.

Reduce the oven temperature to 350°F. Spread the walnuts on a baking tray and bake for 10 minutes or until lightly golden. Keep a close watch on the nuts, as they can burn easily. When cool, roughly chop the walnuts. Combine the watercress, beets, and chives in a large bowl with the dressing and chopped walnuts and serve.

Serves 4

Snow pea salad with Japanese dressing

1 1/2 cups snow peas, trimmed
1 cup snow pea sprouts
1 small red pepper, julienned
1/2 teaspoon dashi granules
1 tablespoon soy sauce
1 tablespoon mirin
1 teaspoon brown sugar
1 garlic clove, crushed
1 teaspoon very finely chopped ginger
1/4 teaspoon sesame oil
1 tablespoon vegetable oil
1 tablespoon toasted sesame seeds

Bring a saucepan of water to a boil, add the snow peas, and cook for 1 minute. Drain, then plunge into a bowl of iced water for 2 minutes. Drain well, then combine with the sprouts and red pepper in a serving bowl.

Dissolve the dashi granules in 1 1/2 tablespoons of hot water and whisk in a small bowl with the soy sauce, mirin, sugar, garlic, ginger, sesame oil, vegetable oil, and half of the toasted sesame seeds. Pour over the snow pea mixture and toss well. Season to taste with salt and pepper, sprinkle with the remaining sesame seeds, and serve.

Serves 4–6

Warm artichoke salad

8 young globe artichokes (7 oz. each)
1 lemon
1/2 cup shredded basil
1/2 cup shaved Parmesan cheese

Dressing
1 garlic clove, finely chopped
1/2 teaspoon sugar
1 teaspoon Dijon mustard
2 teaspoons finely chopped lemon
  zest
1/4 cup lemon juice
1/3 cup extra-virgin olive oil

Remove the tough outer leaves from the artichokes until you get to the pale green leaves. Cut across the top of the artichokes, halfway down the tough leaves, then trim the stems to 1 1/2 inches long and lightly peel them. Cut each artichoke in half lengthwise and remove the inedible flower head in the center with a spoon. Rub each artichoke with lemon while you work and place in a bowl of cold water mixed with lemon juice to keep the artichokes from turning brown.

Place the artichokes in a large saucepan of boiling water, top with a plate or heatproof bowl to keep them immersed, and cook for 25 minutes or until tender. To check tenderness, place a skewer into the largest part of the artichoke. It should insert easily. Drain and cut in half again to serve.

For the dressing, mix the garlic, sugar, mustard, lemon zest, and lemon juice in a pitcher. Season with salt and black pepper, then whisk in the oil with a fork until combined. Pour over the artichokes and sprinkle the basil and Parmesan on top.

Serves 4

Sun-dried tomato and baby spinach salad

2 quarters of preserved lemon
5 cups baby spinach leaves
7 oz. sun-dried tomatoes, sliced
8-oz. jar marinated artichoke hearts,
   drained and sliced
½ cup small black olives
2 tablespoons lemon juice
3 tablespoons olive oil
1 large garlic clove, crushed

Remove and discard the pith and flesh from the preserved lemon. Wash the zest and slice thinly. Place the spinach leaves in a bowl with the sun-dried tomatoes, artichoke hearts, black olives, and the preserved lemon slices.

Place the lemon juice, olive oil, and garlic in a bowl, season to taste with salt and pepper, and mix well. Pour over the spinach mixture and toss to coat. Serve immediately.

Serves 6

Curly endive and garlic crouton salad

Vinaigrette
1 shallot, finely chopped
1 tablespoon Dijon mustard
¼ cup tarragon vinegar
⅔ cup extra-virgin olive oil

1 tablespoon olive oil
½ medium breadstick, sliced
4 whole garlic cloves
1 head curly endive, washed and
  dried
1 cup walnuts, toasted
3½ oz. feta cheese, crumbled

For the vinaigrette, whisk together in a bowl the shallot, mustard, and vinegar. Slowly add the oil, whisking constantly until thickened. Set aside.

Heat the oil in a large frying pan, add the bread and garlic cloves, and cook over medium–high heat for 5–8 minutes or until the bread is crisp. Remove the garlic from the pan. Once the croutons are cool, break into small pieces.

Place the endive, croutons, walnuts, feta cheese, and vinaigrette in a large bowl. Toss together well and serve.

Serves 4–6

Steamed corn salad with Asian dressing

1 large red pepper
3 ears of corn, husks removed
1 cup bean shoots
4 scallions, thinly sliced diagonally

Asian dressing
½ teaspoon crushed garlic
½ teaspoon finely grated fresh ginger
1 teaspoon sugar
1 tablespoon rice vinegar
1 tablespoon soy sauce
1 tablespoon lemon juice
2 teaspoons sesame oil
2 tablespoons peanut oil

Cut the red pepper into large, flat pieces. Cook, skin-side up, under a hot broiler until the skin blackens and blisters. Place in a plastic bag and leave to cool, then peel away the skin and tear the pepper into large strips.

Using a heavy knife, slice the corn into six 1-inch pieces. Steam for 5–8 minutes or until tender. Arrange with the pepper and bean shoots on a serving plate.

For the Asian dressing, mix the garlic, ginger, sugar, rice vinegar, soy sauce, and lemon juice together in a pitcher. Whisk in the oils with a fork until combined and season with black pepper. Drizzle over the salad and top with the scallions.

Serves 4

Eggplant and lentil salad

1/4 cup olive oil
1 large eggplant (10 oz.), diced into
    1/4-inch cubes
1 small red onion, finely diced
1/4 teaspoon ground cumin
3 garlic cloves, chopped
1 cup Puy lentils
1 1/2 cups vegetable stock
2 tablespoons chopped parsley
1 tablespoon red-wine vinegar
1 tablespoon extra-virgin olive oil

Heat 2 tablespoons of the olive oil in a large frying pan over medium heat. Add the eggplant and cook, stirring constantly, for 5 minutes or until soft. Add the onion and cumin and cook for another 2–3 minutes or until the onion has softened. Place the mixture in a bowl and season well with salt and pepper.

Heat the remaining olive oil in the frying pan over medium heat. Add the garlic and cook for 1 minute. Add the lentils and stock and cook, stirring regularly, over low heat for 40 minutes or until the liquid has evaporated and the lentils are tender.

Add the lentils to the bowl with the eggplant and stir in the parsley and red-wine vinegar. Season well with salt and black pepper, drizzle with the extra-virgin olive oil, and serve warm.

Serves 4–6

Coleslaw with lime mayonnaise

2 egg yolks
1 tablespoon soy sauce
1 bird's-eye chili, finely chopped
3 tablespoons lime juice
scant 1 cup olive oil
3 cups shredded purple cabbage
3 cups shredded white cabbage
1 cup grated carrots
2 cups bean sprouts
1 cup cilantro leaves, finely chopped
4 scallions, finely sliced

To make the mayonnaise, place the egg yolks, soy sauce, chili, a pinch of salt, and the lime juice in the bowl of a food processor. With the motor running, very slowly add the olive oil to the egg yolk mixture, a few drops at a time. When about half the oil has been added, add the remaining oil in a steady stream until all has been incorporated. Add 1 tablespoon of warm water and stir well. Place the mayonnaise in a bowl, cover, and refrigerate until needed.

In a large bowl, combine the cabbages, carrots, bean sprouts, cilantro, and scallions. Toss well to combine all the ingredients. Add the lime mayonnaise, stir to combine, and serve.

Serves 4–6

Asparagus orange salad

10½ oz. thin asparagus spears
1½ cups watercress
½ small red onion, very thinly sliced
1 orange, cut into 12 segments
1 tablespoon fresh orange juice
1 teaspoon finely grated orange zest
1 teaspoon sugar
1 tablespoon red-wine vinegar
2 teaspoons poppy seeds
2 tablespoons olive oil
2¼ oz. soft goat cheese

Cook the asparagus in boiling water for 1–2 minutes or until just tender. Rinse under cold water to cool, then combine with the watercress, red onion, and orange segments in a serving dish.

Combine the orange juice, orange zest, sugar, red-wine vinegar, and poppy seeds in a pitcher. Whisk in the oil with a fork until combined and drizzle over the salad. Crumble the goat cheese over the salad and season to taste with salt and pepper.

Serves 4

Red potato salad with dill and mustard dressing

6 medium waxy, red-skinned
 potatoes (2 lb. 8 oz.)

Dill and mustard dressing
1 tablespoon Dijon mustard
1 1/2 tablespoons chopped dill
2 teaspoons brown sugar
1/4 cup red-wine vinegar
1/3 cup olive oil

Steam or boil the potatoes for
20 minutes or until tender. Remove
from the heat, and when cool enough
to handle, cut into 1 1/4-inch chunks.

For the dill and mustard dressing,
mix the mustard, dill, brown sugar,
and vinegar together in a cup. Whisk
in the oil with a fork until combined.
Toss through the warm potatoes
and season with salt and pepper.

Serves 4

Salata baladi (Arabic fresh vegetable salad)

2 tablespoons extra-virgin olive oil
2 tablespoons lemon juice
1 head romaine lettuce, torn into
   bite-size pieces
3 ripe tomatoes, each cut into
   8 pieces
1 green pepper, cut into bite-size
   pieces
1 cucumber, seeded and chopped
6 radishes, sliced
1 small red or Spanish onion, thinly
   sliced
2 tablespoons chopped Italian parsley
2 tablespoons chopped mint

In a bowl, whisk together the olive oil and lemon juice. Season well with salt and pepper.

Combine the vegetables and herbs in a serving bowl and toss well. Add the dressing and toss to combine.

Serves 4–6

Vietnamese salad with lemongrass dressing

7 oz. dried rice vermicelli
1/2 cup torn Vietnamese mint
1/2 cup cilantro leaves
1/2 red onion, cut into thin wedges
1 green mango, julienned
1 cucumber, halved lengthwise and
   thinly sliced diagonally
1 cup crushed peanuts

Lemongrass dressing
1/2 cup lime juice
1 tablespoon brown sugar
1/4 cup seasoned rice vinegar
2 stems lemongrass, finely chopped
2 red chilies, seeded and finely
   chopped
3 kaffir lime leaves, shredded

Place the rice vermicelli in a bowl and cover with boiling water. Leave for 10 minutes or until soft, then drain, rinse under cold water, and cut into short lengths.

Place the vermicelli, mint, cilantro, onion, mango, cucumber, and 3/4 cup of the peanuts in a large bowl and toss together.

To make the dressing, place all the ingredients in a jar with a lid and shake together.

Toss the dressing through the salad and refrigerate for 30 minutes. Sprinkle with the remaining nuts just before serving.

Serves 4–6

Entrées

Artichoke risoni

2 tablespoons butter
1 tablespoon olive oil
2 fennel bulbs, sliced
12-oz. jar marinated artichoke hearts, drained and chopped
1¼ cups cream
1 tablespoon Dijon mustard
3 tablespoons dry white wine
½ cup grated Parmesan cheese
13 oz. risoni (rice-shaped pasta)
2 cups shredded spinach

Heat the butter and oil in a frying pan over medium heat, add the fennel, and cook for 20 minutes or until caramelized. Add the artichoke hearts and cook for another 5–10 minutes. Stir in the cream, mustard, white wine, and grated Parmesan and bring to a boil. Reduce the heat and simmer for 5 minutes.

Meanwhile, cook the risoni in a large saucepan of boiling water until al dente, then drain well.

Add the risoni and spinach to the sauce and cook until the spinach has wilted. This is delicious served with toasted Italian bread.

Serves 4

Baked sweet potato and watercress gnocchi

5 medium orange sweet potatoes
  (1 lb. 9 oz.)
2 medium red potatoes (10 oz.)
3 cups all-purpose flour
1/3 cup grated Parmesan cheese
1 cup watercress leaves, finely
  chopped
1 garlic clove, crushed
4 tablespoons butter
1/4 cup grated Parmesan cheese,
  extra
2 tablespoons chopped parsley

Boil the sweet potatoes and red potatoes in their skins until tender. Drain, then peel when they are cool enough to handle. Press through a ricer into a bowl. Add the flour, grated Parmesan, watercress, and garlic and season well. Gently bring together with your hands until a soft dough forms. To keep the gnocchi tender, it is important not to overwork the dough. Portion into walnut-size pieces and shape using the back of a fork to create the traditional gnocchi shape.

Melt the butter in a large roasting pan. Preheat the broiler to medium–high.

Cook the gnocchi in a large saucepan of boiling salted water for 2 minutes or until they rise to the surface. Scoop out with a slotted spoon, draining off the water. Arrange in the roasting pan, tossing gently in the butter, and grill for 5 minutes or until lightly golden. Sprinkle with the extra Parmesan and chopped parsley and serve immediately.

Serves 6

Couscous vegetable loaf

4 cups vegetable stock
2¼ cups instant couscous
2 tablespoons butter
3 tablespoons olive oil
2 garlic cloves, crushed
1 onion, finely chopped
1 tablespoon ground coriander
1 teaspoon ground cinnamon
1 teaspoon garam masala
9 oz. cherry tomatoes, quartered
1 zucchini, diced
4½-oz. can corn kernels, drained
8 large basil leaves
5½ oz. sun-dried peppers in oil
1 cup chopped basil, extra
⅓ cup orange juice
1 tablespoon lemon juice
3 tablespoons chopped Italian parsley
1 teaspoon honey
1 teaspoon ground cumin

Bring the vegetable stock to a boil in a saucepan. Place the couscous and butter in a bowl, cover with the stock, and leave for 10 minutes.

Meanwhile, heat 1 tablespoon of the oil in a large frying pan and cook the garlic and onion over low heat for 5 minutes or until the onion is soft. Add the spices and cook for 1 minute or until fragrant. Remove from the pan. Add the remaining oil to the pan and cook the tomatoes, zucchini, and corn over high heat until soft.

Line a 12-cup loaf pan with plastic wrap, letting it overhang the sides. Form the basil into two flowers on the base. Drain the peppers, reserving 2 tablespoons of oil, then roughly chop. Add the onion mixture, tomato mixture, pepper, and extra basil to the couscous and mix. Allow to cool.

Press the mixture into the pan and fold the plastic wrap over to cover. Weigh down with food cans and chill overnight.

To make the dressing, place the remaining ingredients and reserved pepper oil in a jar with a lid and shake. Turn out the loaf, cut into slices, and serve with the dressing.

Serves 6

Mushroom risotto

6 cups vegetable stock
2 cups white wine
2 tablespoons olive oil
4 tablespoons butter
1 leek, thinly sliced
1 lb. 2 oz. flat mushrooms, sliced
2¼ cups arborio rice
¾ cup grated Parmesan cheese
3 tablespoons chopped Italian parsley
balsamic vinegar, to serve
shaved Parmesan cheese, to garnish
Italian parsley, to garnish

Place the stock and wine in a large saucepan, bring to a boil, then reduce the heat to low, cover, and keep at a low simmer.

Heat the oil and butter in a large saucepan. Add the leek and cook over medium heat for 5 minutes or until soft and golden. Add the mushrooms and cook for 5 minutes or until tender. Stir in the arborio rice until it is translucent.

Add ½ cup stock, stirring constantly over medium heat until the liquid is absorbed. Continue adding more stock, ½ cup at a time, stirring constantly for 20–25 minutes or until all the stock is absorbed and the rice is tender and creamy.

Stir in the Parmesan and chopped parsley until all the cheese is melted. Serve drizzled with vinegar and top with the shaved Parmesan and parsley.

Serves 4

Eggplant, ricotta, and pasta pots

7 oz. straight macaroni
½ cup light olive oil
1 large eggplant, cut lengthwise
   into ½-inch slices
1 small onion, finely chopped
2 garlic cloves, crushed
14-oz. can diced tomatoes
1¾ cups ricotta cheese
1 cup coarsely grated Parmesan
   cheese
½ cup shredded basil, plus extra
   to garnish

Preheat the oven to 350°F. Cook the macaroni in a large saucepan of boiling water until al dente. Drain.

Heat 2 tablespoons of oil in a nonstick frying pan over medium heat. Cook the eggplant in three batches for 2–3 minutes each side or until golden, adding 2 tablespoons of oil with each batch. Remove and drain well on crumpled paper towels. Add the onion and garlic to the frying pan and cook over medium heat for 2–3 minutes or until just golden. Add the tomatoes and cook for 5 minutes or until the sauce is pulpy and most of the liquid has evaporated. Season with salt and pepper, then remove from the heat.

Combine the ricotta, Parmesan, and basil in a large bowl, then mix in the pasta. Line the base and sides of four 1½-cup ramekins with the eggplant, trimming any overhanging pieces. Top with half the pasta mix, pressing down firmly. Spoon the tomato sauce on top, then cover with the remaining pasta mixture. Bake for 10–15 minutes or until heated through and golden on top. Let stand for 5 minutes, then run a knife around the edges of the ramekins. Invert onto plates and garnish with a sprig of basil.

Serves 4

Frittata of zucchini flowers, oregano, and ricotta salata

2 tablespoons olive oil
1 onion, finely chopped
2 garlic cloves, finely sliced
8 small zucchini with flowers
8 eggs, lightly whisked
¼ cup oregano, chopped
⅓ cup ricotta salata, grated
   (see Note)
¼ cup grated Parmesan cheese
1 tablespoon shaved Parmesan
   cheese
lemon wedges, to serve

Preheat the oven to 400°F. Heat the oil in an ovenproof 8-inch frying pan and cook the onion and garlic until softened. Arrange the zucchini flowers evenly in the pan and add the egg. Sprinkle the oregano, ricotta salata, and grated Parmesan on top and season well with black pepper.

Put the pan in the oven and cook for about 10 minutes or until set. Remove from the oven and allow to cool slightly. Top with the shaved Parmesan, cut into wedges, and serve with a piece of lemon.

Serves 4

Note: Originating in Sicily, ricotta salata is a firm, white, rindless cheese with a nutty, sweet, milky flavor. If unavailable, substitute a mild feta cheese.

Phad Thai

14 oz. flat rice noodles
2 tablespoons peanut oil
2 eggs, lightly beaten
1 onion, cut into thin wedges
2 garlic cloves, crushed
1 small red pepper, cut into thin strips
1/2 cup fried tofu, cut into 1/4-inch-wide strips
6 scallions, thinly sliced diagonally
1/2 cup chopped cilantro leaves
1/4 cup soy sauce
2 tablespoons lime juice
1 tablespoon brown sugar
2 teaspoons sambal oelek
1 cup bean shoots
1/4 cup chopped, roasted, unsalted peanuts

Cook the noodles in a saucepan of boiling water for 5–10 minutes or until tender. Drain and set aside.

Heat a wok over high heat and add enough peanut oil to coat the bottom and side. When smoking, add the eggs and swirl around to form a thin omelette. Cook for 30 seconds or until just set. Roll up, remove, and slice thinly.

Heat the remaining oil in the wok. Cook the onion, garlic, and pepper over high heat for 2–3 minutes or until the onion has softened. Add the noodles, tossing well. Stir in the omelette, tofu, scallions, and half the cilantro.

Pour in the combined soy sauce, lime juice, sugar, and sambal oelek, then toss to coat the noodles. Sprinkle the bean shoots on top and garnish with the peanuts and the remaining cilantro. Serve immediately.

Serves 4

Casareccia pasta with roasted tomatoes, arugula, and goat cheese

16 Roma tomatoes
¼ cup basil leaves, torn
14 oz. casareccia pasta
⅓ cup olive oil
2 garlic cloves, finely sliced
2 tablespoons lemon juice
4 cups arugula, roughly chopped
2 tablespoons chopped parsley
⅓ cup grated Parmesan cheese
3½ oz. goat cheese

Preheat the oven to 315°F. Score a cross in the base of each tomato. Place the tomatoes in a heatproof bowl and cover with boiling water. Leave for 30 seconds, then transfer them to cold water and peel the skin away from the cross. Cut in half and place cut-side up on a wire rack over a baking tray. Season liberally with salt and black pepper and sprinkle the basil leaves on top. Put the tray in the oven and bake for 3 hours.

In a large saucepan of boiling salted water, cook the pasta until al dente. Drain and keep warm.

Heat the olive oil and garlic over low–medium heat until it just begins to sizzle. Remove immediately and add to the pasta with the tomatoes, lemon juice, arugula, parsley, and Parmesan. Stir gently to combine, allowing the heat from the pasta to wilt the arugula. Serve topped with crumbled goat cheese.

Serves 4

Beet ravioli with sage butter sauce

12-oz. jar baby beets in sweet vinegar
1/4 cup grated Parmesan cheese
1 cup ricotta cheese
4 sheets fresh lasagna
fine cornmeal, for sprinkling
1 cup butter, chopped
1/4 cup sage leaves, torn
2 garlic cloves, crushed
shaved Parmesan cheese,
   to garnish

Drain the beets, then grate them into a bowl. Add the Parmesan and ricotta and mix well. Lay a sheet of pasta on a flat surface and place evenly spaced tablespoons of the ricotta mixture on the pasta to make twelve mounds—four across and three down. Flatten the mounds of filling slightly. Lightly brush the edges of the pasta sheet and around each pile of the filling with water.

Place a second sheet of pasta over the top and gently press around each mound to seal and enclose the filling. Using a pasta wheel or sharp knife, cut the pasta into twelve ravioli. Lay them out separately on a lined tray that has been sprinkled with cornmeal. Repeat with the remaining filling and lasagna sheets to make twenty-four ravioli. Gently remove any air bubbles after cutting so that they are completely sealed.

Cook the pasta in a large saucepan of boiling water until al dente. Drain, divide among four serving plates, and keep warm. Melt the butter in a saucepan and cook for 3–4 minutes or until golden brown. Remove from the heat, stir in the sage and garlic, and spoon over the ravioli. Sprinkle with shaved Parmesan and season with ground pepper.

Serves 4

Squash and feta pie

1 lb. 9 oz. butternut squash, cut into
  $3/4$-inch pieces
4 garlic cloves, unpeeled
5 tablespoons olive oil
2 small red onions, halved and sliced
1 tablespoon balsamic vinegar
1 tablespoon brown sugar
$3^1/_2$ oz. feta cheese, broken into
  small pieces
1 tablespoon chopped rosemary
1 large sheet piecrust

Preheat the oven to 400°F. Place the squash and garlic cloves on a baking tray, drizzle with 2 tablespoons olive oil, and bake for 25–30 minutes or until the squash is tender. Transfer the squash to a large bowl and the garlic to a plate. Leave the squash to cool.

Meanwhile, heat 2 tablespoons oil in a pan, add the onion, and cook over medium heat, stirring occasionally, for 10 minutes. Add the vinegar and sugar and cook for 15 minutes or until the onion is caramelized. Remove from the heat and add to the squash. Cool completely.

Add the feta and rosemary to the squash. Squeeze out the garlic flesh and mix it through the vegetables. Season with salt and black pepper.

Roll out the piecrust between two sheets of baking parchment to a 14-inch circle. Remove the top sheet of parchment and place the bottom sheet with the pastry on a tray. Arrange the squash and feta mixture on top, leaving a $1^1/_2$-inch border. Fold over the edges, pleating as you fold, and bake for 30 minutes or until crisp and golden.

Serves 6

Hokkien noodles with Asian greens and glazed tofu

1¼ cups firm tofu (10 oz.)
¼ cup kecap manis
1 tablespoon mushroom soy sauce
1 tablespoon vegetarian oyster sauce
1 teaspoon sesame oil
1 tablespoon peanut oil
2 garlic cloves, crushed
1 tablespoon grated fresh ginger
1 onion, cut into wedges
1 bunch choy sum, roughly chopped
1 bunch baby bok choy, roughly
  chopped
16 oz. fresh hokkien egg noodles,
  separated
2 tablespoons peanut oil, extra

Cut the tofu into ½-inch-thick slices and place in a shallow nonmetallic dish. Mix together the kecap manis, soy sauce, and oyster sauce, and pour over the tofu. Leave to marinate for about 15 minutes, then drain and reserve the marinade.

Heat the oils in a wok over medium heat, add the garlic, ginger, and onion, and stir-fry until the onion is soft. Remove. Add the green vegetables to the wok and stir-fry until just wilted. Remove. Add the separated noodles and the reserved marinade and stir-fry until heated through. Remove from the wok and divide among four plates.

Fry the tofu in the extra oil until it is browned on both sides. Serve the noodles topped with the tofu, green vegetables, and onion mixture.

Serves 4

Zucchini, thyme, and bocconcini pizza

Pizza crust
4 cups all-purpose flour
1/8-oz. package dried yeast
1 teaspoon salt
1 teaspoon sugar
1 tablespoon olive oil

8 zucchini, cut into fine rounds
2 teaspoons grated lemon zest
1/4 cup finely chopped parsley
2 teaspoons thyme sprigs
4 garlic cloves, crushed
4 tablespoons olive oil
1 lb. 2 oz. bocconcini (fresh mozzarella) cheese, finely diced
1/2 cup grated Parmesan cheese
1 tablespoon extra-virgin olive oil

Preheat the oven to 425°F. To make the pizza crust, mix together the flour, yeast, salt, and sugar in a large bowl and make a well in the center. Pour the 1 tablespoon of olive oil and 1 1/4 cups lukewarm water into the well and mix until the flour is incorporated and a soft dough forms. Turn onto a floured countertop and knead for 10 minutes or until the dough is smooth and elastic. Put the dough in a lightly greased bowl, cover with plastic wrap, and leave in a warm place for about 40 minutes or until doubled in size. Punch the dough down, then knead for 1 minute. Divide in half and roll each half out into a 1/4-inch-thick circle. Transfer the crusts to two round pizza trays.

Place the zucchini rounds, lemon zest, parsley, thyme, garlic, and the 4 tablespoons of olive oil in a bowl and mix together. Top each crust evenly with half the bocconcini and half the Parmesan, then top with the zucchini mixture. Evenly distribute the remaining cheese over the top, season well with salt and pepper, and drizzle with the extra-virgin olive oil. Cook for 15–20 minutes or until the base is crisp and the topping is warmed through and golden.

Makes 2

Asparagus and pistachio risotto

4 cups vegetable stock
1 cup white wine
1/3 cup extra-virgin olive oil
1 red onion, finely chopped
2 cups arborio rice
11 oz. asparagus spears, trimmed
    and cut into 1 1/4-inch pieces
1/2 cup cream
1 cup grated Parmesan cheese
1/2 cup shelled pistachio nuts, toasted
    and roughly chopped

Heat the stock and wine in a large saucepan, bring to a boil, then reduce the heat, cover, and keep at a low simmer.

Heat the olive oil in another large saucepan. Add the onion and cook over medium heat for 3 minutes or until soft. Add the rice and stir until the rice is translucent.

Add 1/2 cup of the hot stock and stir constantly over medium heat until the liquid is absorbed. Continue adding more stock, 1/2 cup at a time, stirring constantly for 20–25 minutes or until all the stock is absorbed and the rice is tender and creamy. Add the asparagus during the last 5 minutes of cooking. Remove from the heat.

Let stand for 2 minutes, then stir in the cream and Parmesan and season to taste with salt and black pepper. Serve sprinkled with pistachios.

Serves 4–6

Szechuan-style eggplant

Sauce
1 tablespoon chili paste with garlic
2 tablespoons Chinese rice wine
2 tablespoons soy sauce
½ teaspoon sugar
2 teaspoons Chinese black vinegar
1 cup vegetable stock
½ teaspoon sesame oil

2 tablespoons vegetable oil
1 lb. 2 oz. eggplant, cut into large dice
4 garlic cloves, finely sliced
1 tablespoon julienned ginger
4 scallions, finely sliced diagonally
1 red chili, finely chopped
steamed jasmine rice, to serve

To make the sauce, combine the chili paste, rice wine, soy sauce, sugar, black vinegar, stock, and sesame oil with ½ cup water and mix together well.

Heat a wok over high heat, add the vegetable oil, eggplant, garlic, ginger, scallions, and chili, and stir-fry for 3 minutes. Pour in the sauce, then reduce the heat and cook, covered, for 20 minutes, stirring occasionally, until the eggplant is tender and the sauce has been absorbed.

Serve with steamed jasmine rice.

Serves 4

Penne with tomato and onion jam

¼ cup olive oil
4 red onions, sliced
1 tablespoon brown sugar
2 tablespoons balsamic vinegar
2 (14-oz.) cans tomatoes
1 lb. 2 oz. penne rigate pasta
¾ cup small, pitted black olives or
  pitted and halved kalamata olives
¾ cup grated Parmesan cheese

Heat the oil in a nonstick frying pan over medium heat. Add the onion and sugar and cook for 25–30 minutes or until caramelized.

Stir in the vinegar, bring to a boil, and cook for 5 minutes. Add the tomatoes, return to a boil, then reduce the heat to medium–low and simmer for 25 minutes or until the tomatoes are reduced and jamlike.

Cook the pasta in a large saucepan of rapidly boiling salted water until al dente. Drain, then return to the pan. Add the tomato mixture and olives and stir to combine well. Season to taste with salt and black pepper and garnish with the grated Parmesan.

Serves 4

Notes: Caramelized onions will keep for a few days if covered with oil and stored in the refrigerator. The onions can be combined with goat cheese to make a quick puff pastry tart, or they can be used as a pizza topping.

Bean and pepper stew

1 cup dried kidney beans
2 tablespoons olive oil
2 large garlic cloves, crushed
1 red onion, cut into thin wedges
1 red pepper, cut into $1/2$-inch cubes
1 green pepper, cut into $1/2$-inch cubes
2 (14-oz.) cans chopped tomatoes
2 tablespoons tomato paste
2 cups vegetable stock
2 tablespoons chopped basil
$2/3$ cup kalamata olives, pitted
1–2 teaspoons brown sugar

Put the kidney beans in a large bowl, cover with cold water, and soak overnight. Rinse well, then transfer to a saucepan, cover with cold water, and cook for 45 minutes or until just tender. Drain.

Heat the oil in a saucepan. Cook the garlic and onion over medium heat for 2–3 minutes or until the onion is soft. Add the red and green peppers and cook for another 5 minutes.

Stir in the tomatoes, tomato paste, stock, and beans. Simmer, covered, for 40 minutes or until the beans are cooked through. Stir in the basil, olives, and sugar. Season well with salt and pepper before serving.

Serves 4–6

Butternut squash and spinach lasagna

¼ cup olive oil
3 lb. 5 oz. butternut squash, cut into ½-inch dice
1 lb. 2 oz. spinach leaves, thoroughly washed
4 fresh lasagna sheets, 8 x 5 inches
2 cups ricotta cheese
2 tablespoons cream
¼ cup grated Parmesan cheese
pinch of ground nutmeg

Heat the oil in a nonstick frying pan over medium heat. Add the squash and toss. Cook, stirring occasionally, for 15 minutes or until tender (don't worry if the squash is slightly mashed). Season and keep warm.

Cook the spinach in a large saucepan of boiling water for 30 seconds or until wilted. Using a slotted spoon, transfer to a bowl of cold water. Drain well and squeeze out as much excess water as possible. Finely chop the spinach. Add the lasagna sheets to the pan of boiling water and cook, stirring occasionally, until al dente. Drain and lay the sheets side by side on a clean dish towel. Cut each sheet along its width into thirds.

Put the ricotta, cream, Parmesan, spinach, and nutmeg in a small pan. Stir over low heat for 2–3 minutes or until warmed through. Work quickly to assemble. Place a piece of lasagna on the base of each plate. Using half the squash, top each of the sheets, then cover with another piece of lasagna. Use half the ricotta mixture to spread over the lasagna sheets, then add another lasagna piece. Top with the remaining squash, then with the remaining ricotta mixture. Season well and serve immediately.

Serves 4

Mixed Asian mushrooms with dashi

1 teaspoon dashi granules
1 tablespoon soy sauce
1 tablespoon mirin
1 1/2 tablespoons vegetable oil
1 cup oyster mushrooms, halved if large
2 cups fresh shiitake mushrooms, sliced
2 cups enoki mushrooms, separated into small bunches
1 teaspoon finely grated fresh ginger
1 scallion, white part finely chopped, green part shredded
2 cups shimeji mushrooms, separated

In a small bowl, combine the dashi granules with 1/2 cup boiling water, then stir in the soy sauce and mirin. Set aside.

Heat a wok over high heat, add 1 tablespoon oil, and swirl to coat. Add the oyster, shiitake, and enoki mushrooms in batches and stir-fry for 1–2 minutes or until wilted and softened.

Heat the remaining oil in the wok, add the ginger and white part of the scallion, and stir-fry for 30 seconds or until fragrant. Return all the cooked mushrooms to the wok along with the dashi mixture and allow to come to a boil. Stir-fry for an additional minute or until the mushrooms are heated through. Remove from the heat, add the shimeji mushrooms, and toss through to wilt with the heat from the other mushrooms. Garnish with the scallion greens and serve immediately.

Serves 4

Salad pizza

4 store-bought individual thick
 pizza crusts
2 tablespoons tomato paste
2 teaspoons chopped oregano
2¼ oz. feta cheese, crumbled
⅔ cup grated mozzarella cheese
½ cup grated Parmesan cheese
3 cups arugula leaves, trimmed
3 tablespoons Italian parsley
¼ small red onion, thinly sliced
¼ cup olive oil
1 tablespoon lemon juice
1 teaspoon Dijon mustard
½ cup shaved Parmesan cheese,
 extra

Preheat the oven to 400°F. Place the
pizza crusts on baking sheets. Spread
with tomato paste and sprinkle with
the oregano, feta, and the grated
cheeses. Bake for 12 minutes or until
bubbling.

Meanwhile, combine the arugula,
parsley, and onion in a bowl. Whisk
together the oil, lemon juice, and
mustard and toss through the salad.

Top the pizzas with the salad and
sprinkle with shaved Parmesan.
Season with ground pepper and
serve immediately.

Serves 4

Green curry with sweet potato and eggplant

1 tablespoon vegetable oil
1 onion, chopped
1–2 tablespoons green curry paste (see Note)
1 medium eggplant, quartered and sliced
1³/₄ cups coconut milk
1 cup vegetable stock
6 kaffir lime leaves
1 orange sweet potato, cut into cubes
2 teaspoons brown sugar
2 tablespoons lime juice
2 teaspoons lime zest
cilantro leaves, to garnish

Heat the oil in a large wok or frying pan. Add the onion and curry paste and cook, stirring, over medium heat for 3 minutes. Add the eggplant and cook for another 4–5 minutes or until softened. Pour in the coconut milk and stock, bring to a boil, then reduce the heat and simmer for 5 minutes. Add the lime leaves and sweet potato and cook, stirring occasionally, for 10 minutes or until the vegetables are very tender.

Mix in the sugar, lime juice, and lime zest until well combined with the vegetables. Season to taste with salt. Garnish with fresh cilantro leaves and serve with steamed rice.

Serves 4–6

Note: If this is to be a vegetarian meal, make sure you choose a green curry paste that does not contain shrimp paste.

Roasted chunky ratatouille cannelloni

1 medium eggplant
2 zucchini
1 large red pepper
1 large green pepper
3–4 ripe Roma tomatoes
12 unpeeled garlic cloves
3 tablespoons olive oil
1$\frac{1}{4}$ cups tomato pasta sauce
12 oz. cannelloni tubes
3 tablespoons shredded basil
1$\frac{1}{4}$ cups ricotta cheese
3$\frac{1}{2}$ oz. feta cheese
1 egg, lightly beaten
1$\frac{3}{4}$ oz. pecorino pepato cheese, grated

Preheat the oven to 400°F. Cut the eggplant, zucchini, peppers, and tomatoes into $\frac{3}{4}$-inch cubes and place in a baking dish with the garlic. Drizzle with the oil and toss to coat. Bake for 1 hour 30 minutes or until the vegetables are tender and the tomatoes slightly mushy. Peel and lightly mash the garlic cloves.

Pour the pasta sauce over the base of a large ovenproof dish. Spoon the ratatouille into the cannelloni tubes and arrange in the dish.

Combine the basil, ricotta, feta, and egg, season well, and spoon over the cannelloni. Sprinkle with the pecorino and bake for 30 minutes or until the cannelloni is soft.

Serves 6–8

Tofu, snow pea, and mushroom stir-fry

1 1/4 cups jasmine rice
1/4 cup peanut oil
1 lb. 5 oz. firm tofu, drained, cut
  into 3/4-inch cubes
2 teaspoons sambal oelek or chili
  paste
2 garlic cloves, finely chopped
14 oz. fresh Asian mushrooms
  (shiitake, oyster, or black fungus),
  sliced
1 1/2 cups snow peas, trimmed
1/4 cup kecap manis

Bring a large saucepan of water to a boil. Add the rice and cook for 12 minutes, stirring occasionally. Drain well.

Meanwhile, heat a wok until very hot. Add 2 tablespoons of the peanut oil and swirl to coat. Add the tofu in two batches and stir-fry on all sides for 2–3 minutes or until lightly browned. Transfer to a plate.

Heat the remaining oil in the wok, add the sambal oelek, garlic, mushrooms, snow peas, and 1 tablespoon water, and stir-fry for 1–2 minutes or until the vegetables are almost cooked but still crunchy.

Return the tofu to the wok, add the kecap manis, and stir-fry for 1 minute or until heated through and well combined. Serve immediately with the jasmine rice.

Serves 4

Notes: Firm tofu is good for stir-frying, as it will hold its shape. As a variation, use 1 tablespoon grated fresh ginger instead of sambal oelek.

Fusilli with broccolini, chili, and olives

3 tablespoons olive oil
1 onion, finely chopped
3 garlic cloves
1 teaspoon chili flakes
1 lb. 9 oz. broccolini (baby broccoli), cut into 1/2-inch pieces
1/2 cup vegetable stock
14 oz. fusilli pasta
1/2 cup black olives, pitted and chopped
1/4 cup finely chopped parsley
1/4 cup grated pecorino cheese
2 tablespoons basil leaves, shredded

Heat the olive oil in a large nonstick frying pan over medium heat. Cook the onion, garlic, and chili until softened, then add the broccolini and cook for 5 minutes. Pour in the stock and cook, covered, for 5 minutes.

Meanwhile, cook the fusilli in a large saucepan of rapidly boiling water until al dente. Drain and keep warm.

When the broccolini is tender, remove from the heat. Add to the pasta with the olives, parsley, pecorino, and basil and season well. Gently toss together and serve immediately.

Serves 4

Rustic Greek pie

1-lb. package frozen spinach, thawed
1 frozen piecrust, thawed
3 garlic cloves, finely chopped
5½ oz. haloumi cheese, grated
4½ oz. feta cheese, crumbled
1 tablespoon oregano sprigs
2 eggs
¼ cup cream
lemon wedges, to serve

Preheat the oven to 415°F. Squeeze the excess liquid from the spinach.

Place the piecrust on a baking sheet and spread the spinach in the middle, leaving a 1¼-inch border around the edge. Sprinkle the garlic over the spinach and pile the haloumi and feta on top. Sprinkle with oregano and season well. Cut a short slit into each corner of the crust, then tuck each side of the crust over to form a border around the filling.

Lightly beat the eggs with the cream and carefully pour the egg mixture over the spinach filling. Bake for 30–40 minutes or until the crust is golden and the filling is set. Serve with the lemon wedges.

Serves 4

Sweet ginger and chili vegetables with rice noodles

1 lb. 2 oz. fresh rice noodle sheets,
   at room temperature
2 tablespoons vegetable oil
1 teaspoon sesame oil
3 tablespoons grated fresh ginger
1 onion, thinly sliced
1 red pepper, sliced
3/4 cup fresh shiitake mushrooms,
   sliced
1 cup baby corn, halved
1 lb. 2 oz. Chinese broccoli (gai larn),
   sliced
1 cup snow peas
3 tablespoons sweet chili sauce
2 tablespoons light soy sauce
2 tablespoons dark soy sauce
1 tablespoon lime juice
16 Thai basil leaves

Cut the noodle sheets into 1 1/4-inch-wide strips, then cut each strip into three. Gently separate the noodles (you may need to run a little cold water over them to do this).

Heat the oils in a wok, add the ginger and onion, and stir-fry until the onion is soft. Add the vegetables and stir-fry until brightly colored and just tender.

Add the noodles to the vegetables and stir-fry until the noodles start to soften. Stir in the combined sauces and lime juice and cook until heated through. Remove from the heat, toss in the basil leaves, and serve.

Serves 4

Zucchini pasta bake

7 oz. risoni (rice-shaped pasta)
3 tablespoons butter
4 scallions, thinly sliced
2 zucchini (14 oz.), grated
4 eggs
1/2 cup cream
1/2 cup ricotta cheese (see Note)
2/3 cup grated mozzarella cheese
3/4 cup grated Parmesan cheese

Preheat the oven to 350°F. Cook the pasta in a large saucepan of rapidly boiling water until al dente. Drain well.

Meanwhile, heat the butter in a frying pan, add the scallions, and cook for 1 minute, then add the zucchini and cook for another 4 minutes or until soft. Cool slightly.

Combine the eggs, cream, ricotta, mozzarella, risoni, and half of the Parmesan, then stir in the zucchini mixture. Season well. Spoon into four 1/2-quart greased ovenproof dishes, but not to the brim. Sprinkle with the remaining Parmesan and cook for 25–30 minutes or until firm and golden.

Serves 4

Note: With such simple flavors, it is important to use good-quality fresh ricotta from the deli section of your local supermarket.

Eggplant and mushroom skewers with tomato concassé

12 long rosemary sprigs
18 Swiss brown mushrooms
1 small eggplant, cut into ¾-inch cubes
¼ cup olive oil
2 tablespoons balsamic vinegar
2 garlic cloves, crushed
1 teaspoon sugar
olive oil, for brushing
sea salt, to sprinkle (optional)

Tomato concassé
5 medium tomatoes
1 tablespoon olive oil
1 small onion, finely chopped
1 garlic clove, crushed
1 tablespoon tomato paste
2 teaspoons sugar
2 teaspoons balsamic vinegar
1 tablespoon chopped Italian parsley

Remove the leaves from the rosemary sprigs, leaving 2 inches on the tips. Reserve 1 tablespoon of the leaves. Cut the mushrooms in half, stems intact. Place the mushrooms and eggplant in a nonmetallic bowl. Add the combined oil, vinegar, garlic, and sugar, then season and toss. Marinate for 15 minutes.

Score a cross in the base of each tomato. Put in a bowl of boiling water for 30 seconds, then plunge into cold water. Peel the skin away from the cross. Cut in half and scoop out the seeds with a spoon. Dice the flesh. Heat the oil in a saucepan over medium heat. Cook the onion and garlic for 2–3 minutes or until soft. Reduce the heat and add the tomatoes, tomato paste, sugar, vinegar, and parsley. Simmer for 10 minutes or until the liquid has evaporated. Keep warm.

Thread alternating mushroom and eggplant pieces onto the rosemary sprigs (three mushroom halves and two cubes of eggplant on each sprig). Lightly oil a grilling pan and cook the skewers for 7–8 minutes or until the eggplant is tender, turning occasionally. Serve with the concassé and sprinkle with salt and rosemary.

Serves 4

Soybean moussaka

2 eggplants
1 tablespoon vegetable oil
1 onion, finely chopped
2 garlic cloves, crushed
2 ripe tomatoes, peeled, seeded,
   and chopped
2 teaspoons tomato paste
1/2 teaspoon dried oregano
1/2 cup dry white wine
10 1/2-oz. can soybeans, rinsed and
   drained
3 tablespoons chopped Italian parsley
2 tablespoons butter
2 tablespoons all-purpose flour
pinch of ground nutmeg
1 1/4 cups milk
1/3 cup grated cheddar cheese

Preheat the oven to 350°F. Cut the eggplants in half lengthwise. Spoon out the flesh, leaving a 1/2-inch border and place on a large baking tray, cut-side up. Use crumpled foil around the sides of the eggplant to support it.

Heat the oil in a frying pan. Cook the onion and garlic over medium heat for 3 minutes or until soft. Add the tomato, tomato paste, oregano, and wine. Bring to a boil and cook for 3 minutes or until the liquid is reduced and the tomatoes are soft. Stir in the soybeans and parsley.

To make the sauce, melt the butter in a saucepan. Stir in the flour and cook over medium heat for 1 minute or until pale and foamy. Remove from the heat and gradually stir in the nutmeg and milk. Return to the heat and stir constantly until the sauce boils and thickens. Pour a third of the white sauce into the tomato mixture and stir well.

Spoon the mixture into the eggplant shells. Smooth the surface before spreading the remaining sauce evenly over the top and sprinkling with cheese. Bake for 50 minutes or until cooked through. Serve hot.

Serves 4

Conchiglie rigate with spring vegetables

1 lb. 2 oz. conchiglie rigate (small pasta shells)
2 cups frozen peas
2 cups frozen fava beans, blanched and peeled
⅓ cup olive oil
6 scallions, cut into 1¼-inch pieces
2 garlic cloves, finely chopped
1 cup vegetable or chicken stock
12 thin, fresh asparagus spears, cut into 2-inch lengths
½ teaspoon finely grated lemon zest
¼ cup lemon juice
shaved Parmesan cheese, to garnish

Cook the pasta in a large saucepan of boiling water until al dente. Drain, then return to the pan. Meanwhile, place the peas in a saucepan of boiling water and cook them for 1–2 minutes or until tender. Remove with a slotted spoon and plunge into cold water. Add the fava beans to the same saucepan of boiling water and cook for 1–2 minutes, then drain and plunge into cold water. Remove and slip the skins off the beans.

Heat 2 tablespoons of the oil in a frying pan. Add the scallions and garlic and cook over medium heat for 2 minutes or until softened. Pour in the stock and cook for 5 minutes or until slightly reduced. Add the asparagus and cook for 3–4 minutes or until bright green and just tender. Stir in the peas and fava beans and cook for 2–3 minutes or until heated through.

Toss the remaining oil through the pasta, then add the vegetables, lemon zest, and lemon juice. Season and toss together well. Serve topped with shaved Parmesan.

Serves 4

Orange sweet potato, spinach, and water chestnut stir-fry

1 1/2 cups long-grain rice
4 medium orange sweet potatoes
  (1 lb. 2 oz.)
1 tablespoon vegetable oil
2 garlic cloves, crushed
2 teaspoons sambal oelek
  (see Notes)
8-oz. can water chestnuts, sliced
2 teaspoons brown sugar
14 oz. spinach, stems removed
2 tablespoons soy sauce
2 tablespoons vegetable stock

Bring a large saucepan of water to a boil. Add the rice and cook for 12 minutes, stirring occasionally. Drain well.

Meanwhile, cut the sweet potatoes into 1/2-inch cubes and cook in a large saucepan of boiling water for 15 minutes or until tender. Drain well.

Heat a wok until very hot, add the oil, and swirl to coat. Stir-fry the garlic and sambal oelek for 1 minute or until fragrant. Add the sweet potatoes and water chestnuts and stir-fry over medium–high heat for 2 minutes. Reduce the heat to medium, add the brown sugar, and cook for another 2 minutes or until the sugar has melted. Add the spinach, soy sauce, and stock and toss until the spinach has just wilted. Serve on a bed of steamed rice.

Serves 4

Notes: Sambal oelek is made from mashed fresh red chilies mixed with salt and vinegar or tamarind.

Mushroom potpies

5 tablespoons olive oil
1 leek, sliced
1 garlic clove, crushed
2 lb. 4 oz. large field mushrooms,
   roughly chopped
1 teaspoon chopped thyme
1¼ cups cream
1 sheet puff pastry, thawed
1 egg yolk, beaten, to glaze

Preheat the oven to 350°F. Heat 1 tablespoon of the oil in a frying pan over medium heat. Cook the leek and garlic for 5 minutes or until the leek is soft and translucent. Transfer to a large saucepan.

Heat the remaining oil in the frying pan over high heat and cook the mushrooms in two batches, stirring frequently, for 5–7 minutes per batch or until the mushrooms have released their juices and are soft and slightly colored. Transfer to the saucepan, then add the thyme.

Place the saucepan over high heat and stir in the cream. Cook, stirring occasionally, for 7–8 minutes or until the cream has reduced to a thick sauce. Remove from the heat and season well with salt and pepper.

Divide the filling among four 1¼-cup ramekins. Cut the pastry into rounds slightly larger than the ramekins. Brush the rims of the ramekins with a little of the egg yolk, place the pastries on top, and press down on the edges to seal. Brush the tops with the remaining egg yolk. Place the ramekins on a baking sheet. Bake for 20–25 minutes or until the pastry has risen and is golden brown.

Serves 4

Fusilli with roasted tomatoes, tapenade, and bocconcini

1 lb. 12 oz. cherry tomatoes, halved
   if they are large
1 lb. 2 oz. fusilli pasta
10½ oz. bocconcini (fresh mozzarella)
   cheese, sliced
1 tablespoon chopped thyme

Tapenade
1½ tablespoons capers
2 small garlic cloves
1½ cups sliced black olives
3 tablespoons lemon juice
4–5 tablespoons extra-virgin
   olive oil

Preheat the oven to 400°F. Place the tomatoes on a baking tray, sprinkle with salt and pepper, and bake for 10 minutes or until slightly dried.

To make the tapenade, place the capers, garlic, olives, and lemon juice in a food processor and mix together. With the motor running, gradually add the oil until the mixture forms a smooth paste.

Cook the pasta in a large saucepan of rapidly boiling water until al dente, then drain.

Toss the tapenade and bocconcini through the hot pasta. Top with the roasted tomatoes and thyme and serve immediately.

Serves 4–6

Rice and red lentil pilaf

Garam masala
1 tablespoon coriander seeds
1 tablespoon cardamom pods
1 tablespoon cumin seeds
1 teaspoon whole black peppercorns
1 teaspoon whole cloves
1 small cinnamon stick, crushed

¼ cup vegetable oil
1 onion, chopped
3 garlic cloves, chopped
1 cup basmati rice
1 cup red lentils
3 cups hot vegetable stock
scallions, sliced diagonally, to garnish

To make the garam masala, place all the spices in a frying pan and dry-fry over medium heat for 1 minute or until fragrant. Blend to a fine powder in a spice grinder or blender.

Heat the oil in a saucepan. Add the onion, garlic, and 1 tablespoon garam masala. Cook over medium heat for 3 minutes or until the onion is soft.

Stir in the rice and lentils and cook for 2 minutes. Add the stock and stir well. Slowly bring to a boil, then reduce the heat and simmer, covered, for 15–20 minutes or until the rice is cooked and all the stock has been absorbed. Gently fluff the rice with a fork. Garnish with scallions.

Serves 4–6

Note: If you prefer, you can use store-bought garam masala instead of making it.

Tamari roasted almonds with spicy green beans

3 tablespoons sesame oil
2½ cups jasmine rice
1 long red chili, seeded and finely
  chopped
¾-inch piece ginger, peeled and
  grated
2 garlic cloves, crushed
2½ cups green beans, cut into
  2-inch lengths
½ cup hoisin sauce
1 tablespoon brown sugar
2 tablespoons mirin
1 cup tamari roasted almonds,
  roughly chopped (see Note)

Preheat the oven to 400°F. Heat 1 tablespoon of oil in a 6-cup ovenproof dish, add the rice, and stir until well coated. Stir in 4 cups boiling water. Cover and bake for 20 minutes or until all the water is absorbed. Keep warm.

Meanwhile, heat the remaining oil in a wok or large frying pan and cook the chili, ginger, and garlic for 1 minute or until lightly browned. Add the beans, hoisin sauce, and sugar and stir-fry for 2 minutes. Stir in the mirin and cook for 1 minute or until the beans are tender but still crunchy.

Remove from the heat and stir in the almonds just before serving. Serve with the rice.

Serves 4–6

Note: Tamari roasted almonds can be found in some health food stores. If unavailable, soak unpeeled almonds in tamari for 30 minutes. Drain and dry with paper towels. Heat 1 tablespoon oil in a nonstick frying pan. Toss the almonds for 2–3 minutes, then drain.

Somen noodle nests with eggplant and shiitake mushrooms

2 small eggplants, cut into ½-inch-
  thick slices
12 dried shiitake mushrooms
¼ cup vegetable oil
1 cup fresh enoki mushrooms
1 teaspoon dashi granules
1 tablespoon sugar
1 tablespoon white miso
1 tablespoon mirin (sweet rice wine)
¼ cup Japanese soy sauce
11 oz. dried somen noodles

Blanch the eggplants in boiling water for 5 minutes. Drain, then transfer to a plate and weigh down with another plate for 15 minutes to press out any remaining liquid. Pat dry.

Soak the dried shiitake mushrooms in 1 cup boiling water for 10 minutes. Drain and reserve the liquid. Heat the oil in a large frying pan and cook the eggplant slices in batches until golden brown on both sides. Remove. Add the enoki mushrooms and cook for 10 seconds. Remove. Stir in the dashi, sugar, miso, mirin, soy sauce, reserved mushroom liquid, shiitake mushrooms, and ½ cup water. Bring to a boil, then cover and simmer for 10 minutes.

Cook the somen noodles in boiling water for 3 minutes or until tender. Drain well.

Place nests of the noodles onto plates, top with eggplant slices and the mushrooms, and drizzle with the sauce. Serve immediately.

Serves 4

Conchiglioni stuffed with roast squash and ricotta

2 lb. 4 oz. butternut squash, cut into
  large wedges
olive oil, to drizzle
10 unpeeled garlic cloves
2 1/4 cups ricotta cheese
1/3 cup finely shredded basil
3 cups tomato pasta sauce
1/2 cup dry white wine
32 conchiglioni rigati (large pasta
  shells)
1 cup grated Parmesan cheese

.

Preheat the oven to 400°F. Place the squash in a baking dish, drizzle with olive oil, and season. Bake for 30 minutes, then add the garlic and bake for another 15 minutes or until tender. Cool slightly, then peel and mash the squash and garlic. Mix with the ricotta and half the basil and season to taste.

Put the pasta sauce and wine in a saucepan, bring to a boil, then reduce the heat and simmer for 10 minutes or until slightly thickened.

Cook the pasta in rapidly boiling water until al dente. Lay out on paper towels to dry, then fill with the squash mixture. Spread any remaining filling in a large ovenproof dish, top with the shells, and pour on the sauce. Sprinkle with Parmesan and the remaining basil and bake for about 30 minutes.

Serves 6

Spaghetti with lemon and arugula

13 oz. spaghetti
2 cups arugula, finely shredded
1 tablespoon finely chopped lemon
  zest
1 garlic clove, finely chopped
1 small red chili, seeded and finely
  chopped
1 teaspoon chili oil
5 tablespoons extra-virgin olive oil
½ cup finely grated Parmesan cheese

Cook the spaghetti until al dente. Drain well.

Combine the arugula, lemon zest, garlic, chili, chili oil, extra-virgin olive oil, and two-thirds of the grated Parmesan in a large bowl and mix together gently.

Add the pasta to the arugula and lemon mixture and stir together well. Serve topped with the remaining Parmesan and season to taste with salt and cracked black pepper.

Serves 4

Note: If you prefer, you can substitute basil leaves for the arugula.

Green stir-fry with sesame and soy

2 tablespoons light soy sauce
1 tablespoon hoisin sauce
1 tablespoon vegetable or chicken
  stock
2 tablespoons vegetable oil
1 teaspoon sesame oil
4 garlic cloves, finely sliced
2 teaspoons julienned ginger
4 bunches baby bok choy, cut into
  quarters, well washed, and drained
1 cup snow peas, trimmed
1 cup sugar snap peas, trimmed
2 tablespoons bamboo shoots,
  julienned
jasmine rice, to serve

In a small cup, mix together the light soy sauce, hoisin sauce, and stock.

Heat a wok over high heat and add the vegetable and sesame oils. Stir-fry the garlic, ginger, and bok choy for 3 minutes. Add the snow peas, sugar snap peas, and bamboo shoots and stir-fry for another 5 minutes. Pour in the sauce and gently toss until the sauce has reduced slightly to coat the just-tender vegetables. Serve immediately with jasmine rice.

Serves 4

Potato and zucchini casserole

1 large red pepper
¼ cup olive oil
2 onions, sliced
2 garlic cloves, crushed
3 zucchini (14 oz.), thickly sliced
3 medium waxy (e.g., red, pink fir) potatoes (14 oz.), unpeeled, cut into ½-inch slices
6 medium tomatoes, peeled and roughly chopped
1 teaspoon dried oregano
2 tablespoons chopped Italian parsley
2 tablespoons chopped dill
½ teaspoon ground cinnamon

Preheat the oven to 350°F. Remove the seeds and membrane from the red pepper and cut the flesh into squares.

Heat 2 tablespoons of the olive oil in a heavy-based frying pan over medium heat. Cook the onion, stirring frequently, for 10 minutes. Add the garlic and cook for another 2 minutes. Place all the other ingredients in a large bowl and season generously with salt and black pepper. Add the softened onion and garlic and toss everything together. Transfer to a large baking dish and drizzle the remaining oil over the vegetables.

Cover and bake for 1–1½ hours or until the vegetables are tender, stirring every 30 minutes. Check for doneness by inserting the point of a small knife into the potatoes. When the potatoes flake easily, the potatoes are cooked.

Serves 4–6

Pearl barley and Asian mushroom pilaf

1½ cups pearl barley
3 dried shiitake mushrooms
2½ cups vegetable or chicken stock
½ cup dry sherry
2 tablespoons olive oil
1 large onion, finely chopped
3 garlic cloves, crushed
2 tablespoons grated fresh ginger
1 teaspoon Szechuan peppercorns, crushed
1 lb. 2 oz. mixed fresh Asian mushrooms (oyster, Swiss brown, enoki)
13 oz. choy sum, cut into short lengths
1 tablespoon kecap manis
1 teaspoon sesame oil

Soak the pearl barley in enough cold water to cover for at least 6 hours or, preferably, overnight. Drain.

Soak the shiitake mushrooms in enough boiling water to cover for 15 minutes. Strain, reserving ½ cup of the liquid. Discard the stalks and finely slice the caps.

Heat the stock and sherry in a small saucepan. Cover and keep at a low simmer.

Heat the oil in a large saucepan over medium heat. Cook the onion for 4–5 minutes or until softened. Add the garlic, ginger, and peppercorns and cook for 1 minute. Slice the Asian mushrooms, reserving the enoki for later. Increase the heat and add the mushrooms. Cook for 5 minutes or until the mushrooms have softened. Add the barley, shiitake mushrooms, reserved soaking liquid, and hot stock. Stir well to combine. Bring to a boil, then reduce the heat to low and simmer, covered, for 35 minutes or until the liquid evaporates.

Steam the choy sum until just wilted. Add to the barley mixture with the enoki mushrooms. Stir in the kecap manis and sesame oil and serve.

Serves 4

Balsamic pepper on angel-hair pasta

10½ oz. angel-hair pasta
2 red peppers
2 yellow peppers
2 green peppers
4 garlic cloves, crushed
2 tablespoons orange juice
⅓ cup balsamic vinegar
3½ oz. goat cheese
½ cup basil

Cook the pasta in a large saucepan of rapidly boiling water until al dente. Drain well.

Cut the peppers into large, flat pieces and place under a hot broiler until the skin blisters and blackens. Leave to cool in a plastic bag, then peel away the skin and cut the flesh into thin strips.

Combine the pepper strips, garlic, orange juice, and balsamic vinegar. Drizzle over the pasta and toss gently.

Serve topped with crumbled goat cheese and basil and a sprinkling of cracked black pepper.

Serves 4

Vegetable pasta torte

4 small Roma tomatoes
2 medium orange sweet potatoes
(10 oz.), peeled and cut into large
chunks
1 red pepper
3 tablespoons vegetable oil
7 oz. fettucine
6 eggs, lightly beaten
1 cup milk
1 cup grated cheddar cheese
1/2 cup Italian parsley leaves
7 oz. feta cheese, cut into large
cubes

Preheat the oven to 400°F. Place the whole tomatoes, sweet potatoes, and pepper in a baking dish, drizzle with oil, and season well. Bake for 40 minutes or until tender.

Peel the pepper and cut it into large chunks.

Cook the pasta in rapidly boiling water until al dente, then drain well. Combine the egg, milk, and cheddar.

Arrange half the vegetables and half the parsley in a greased 10-inch nonstick frying pan with deep sides. Top with half the pasta and feta, then layer with the remaining vegetables, parsley, pasta, and feta. Top with the egg mix. Cook over medium heat for 15–20 minutes or until just set (be careful not to burn the base). Cook under a broiler for another 15–20 minutes or until the top is golden brown. Leave for 5 minutes before turning out to serve.

Serves 6–8

Yellow curry of squash with green beans and cashews

2 cups coconut cream (do not shake the can)
1 tablespoon yellow curry paste
1/2 cup vegetable or chicken stock
1 lb. 2 oz. Japanese squash, peeled and diced
2 cups green beans, trimmed and cut in half
2 tablespoons soy sauce
2 tablespoons lime juice
1 tablespoon brown sugar
1/4 cup cilantro leaves
1/4 cup cashews, toasted
steamed jasmine rice, to serve

Spoon the thick coconut cream from the top of the can into the wok and heat until boiling. Add the curry paste, then reduce the heat and simmer, stirring, for 5 minutes, until the oil begins to separate.

Add the remaining coconut cream, stock, and squash and simmer for 10 minutes. Add the green beans and cook for another 8 minutes or until the vegetables are tender.

Gently stir in the soy sauce, lime juice, and brown sugar. Garnish with the cilantro leaves and cashews and serve with steamed jasmine rice.

Serves 4

Sweet potato and sage risotto

1/4 cup extra-virgin olive oil
1 red onion, cut into thin wedges
4 medium orange sweet potatoes
   (1 lb. 5 oz.), peeled and cut into
   3/4-inch cubes
2 cups arborio rice
5 cups hot vegetable stock
3/4 cup shredded Parmesan cheese
3 tablespoons shredded sage
shaved Parmesan cheese, extra,
   to garnish

Heat 3 tablespoons oil in a large saucepan and cook the onion over medium heat for 2–3 minutes or until softened. Add the sweet potatoes and rice and stir until well coated in the oil.

Add 1/2 cup of the hot stock, stirring constantly over medium heat until the liquid is absorbed. Continue adding more stock, 1/2 cup at a time, stirring constantly for 20–25 minutes or until all the stock is absorbed, the sweet potatoes are cooked, and the rice is tender and creamy.

Add the Parmesan and 2 tablespoons of the sage. Season well and stir to combine. Spoon into four bowls and drizzle with the remaining oil. Sprinkle the remaining sage on top and garnish with shaved Parmesan.

Serves 4

Orecchiette with broccoli

1 lb. 10 oz. broccoli, cut into florets
1 lb. orecchiette (small, ear-shaped
pasta)
¼ cup extra-virgin olive oil
½ teaspoon dried chili flakes
⅓ cup grated pecorino or Parmesan
cheese

Cook the broccoli in a saucepan of boiling salted water for 5 minutes or until just tender. Remove with a slotted spoon, drain well, and return the water to a boil. Cook the pasta in the boiling water until al dente, then drain well and return to the pan.

Meanwhile, heat the oil in a heavy-based frying pan and add the chili flakes and broccoli. Increase the heat to medium and cook, stirring, for 5 minutes or until the broccoli is well coated and beginning to break apart. Season. Add to the pasta, toss in the cheese, and serve.

Serves 6

Balti eggplant and tofu stir-fry

2 tablespoons vegetable oil
1 onion, finely chopped
¼ cup balti curry paste
10½ oz. slender eggplant, cut
   diagonally into ½-inch slices
10½ oz. firm tofu, cut into ½-inch
   cubes
3 ripe tomatoes, cut into wedges
¼ cup vegetable stock
2 cups baby spinach leaves
⅓ cup toasted cashews
saffron rice, to serve

Heat a wok or deep frying pan until
very hot. Add the oil and swirl to coat.
Add the onion and stir-fry over high
heat for 3–4 minutes or until softened
and golden.

Stir in the balti curry paste and cook
for 1 minute. Add the eggplant and
cook for 5 minutes. Stir in the tofu,
gently tossing for 3–4 minutes or
until golden.

Add the tomatoes and stock and
cook for 3 minutes or until the
tomatoes are soft. Stir in the spinach
and cook for 1–2 minutes or until
wilted. Season. Sprinkle the cashews
on top and serve with saffron rice.

Serves 4

Mushroom long-life noodles

14 oz. pancit canton noodles or
egg noodles
1 tablespoon peanut oil
3 tablespoons soy sauce
1½ tablespoons mushroom soy
sauce
1 teaspoon sesame oil
1 teaspoon sugar
1 cup vegetable stock
1 tablespoon grated fresh ginger
2 garlic cloves, crushed
9 oz. shiitake mushrooms, sliced
9 oz. hon-shimeji mushrooms,
separated
4½ oz. wood ear fungus, sliced
(see Note)
9 oz. enoki mushrooms, separated
½ cup scallions, finely sliced
diagonally

Bring a saucepan of water to a boil and cook the noodles for 3 minutes. Drain, rinse the noodles under cold water, then drain again. Toss the noodles with 1 teaspoon of peanut oil.

In a small bowl, thoroughly mix together the soy sauce, mushroom soy sauce, sesame oil, sugar, and vegetable stock.

In a wok, heat the remaining peanut oil over high heat, add the ginger and garlic, and stir-fry for 1 minute. Add the shiitake mushrooms, shimeji mushrooms, and wood ear fungus and stir-fry for 3 minutes. Add the noodles, enoki mushrooms, scallions, and combined sauce ingredients. Gently toss, cooking until the noodles have absorbed the sauce.

Serves 4

Note: Wood ear fungus is a type of mushroom that is sold dried; when reconstituted, they increase several times in size and look like ears. They are believed by many to be good for the heart. Look for them in Asian markets.

Fettucine with creamy spinach and roast tomatoes

6 Roma tomatoes
3 tablespoons butter
2 garlic cloves, crushed
1 onion, chopped
1 lb. 2 oz. spinach, trimmed
1 cup vegetable stock
1/2 cup heavy cream
1 lb. 2 oz. fresh spinach fettucine
1/2 cup shaved Parmesan cheese

Preheat the oven to 425°F. Cut the tomatoes in half lengthwise, then cut each half into three wedges. Place the wedges on a lightly greased baking tray and bake for 30–35 minutes or until softened and slightly golden.

Meanwhile, heat the butter in a large frying pan. Add the garlic and onion and cook over medium heat for 5 minutes or until the onion is soft. Add the spinach, stock, and cream, increase the heat to high, and bring to a boil. Simmer rapidly for 5 minutes.

While the spinach mixture is cooking, cook the pasta in a large saucepan of boiling water until al dente. Drain and return to the pan. Remove the spinach mixture from the heat and season well. Cool slightly, then process in a food processor until smooth. Toss through the pasta until well coated. Divide among serving bowls, top with the roasted tomatoes and Parmesan, and serve.

Serves 4–6

Italian zucchini pie

5 medium zucchini (1 lb. 5 oz.),
　　grated and mixed with
　　¼ teaspoon salt
5½ oz. provolone cheese, grated
½ cup ricotta cheese
3 eggs
2 garlic cloves, crushed
2 teaspoons finely chopped basil
pinch of ground nutmeg
2 sheets prepared piecrust
1 egg, extra, lightly beaten

Preheat the oven to 400°F and heat a baking sheet. Grease a 9-inch pie dish. Drain the zucchini in a colander for 30 minutes, then squeeze out any excess liquid. Place in a bowl with the cheeses, eggs, garlic, basil, and nutmeg. Season and mix well.

Using two-thirds of the piecrust, line the base and sides of the dish. Spoon the filling into the piecrust and level the surface. Brush the exposed rim of the piecrust with egg. Use two-thirds of the remaining piecrust to make a lid. Cover the filling with it, pressing the edges together firmly. Trim the edges and reserve the scraps. Crimp the rim. Prick the top all over with a fork and brush with egg.

From the remaining piecrust, cut a strip about 12 x 4 inches. Cut this into nine strips about ½ inch wide. Press three strips together at one end and press onto the countertop. Plait the ropes. Make two more plaits, trim the ends, and space the plaits parallel across the center of the pie. Brush with egg. Bake on the hot baking sheet for 50 minutes or until golden.

Serves 6

Sweet potato ravioli

4 medium orange sweet potatoes
  (1 lb. 2 oz.), chopped
2 teaspoons lemon juice
3/4 cup butter
1/2 cup grated Parmesan cheese
1 tablespoon chopped chives
1 egg, lightly beaten
9-oz. package wonton wrappers
2 tablespoons sage, torn
2 tablespoons chopped walnuts

Cook the sweet potatoes and lemon juice in boiling water for 15 minutes or until tender. Drain and pat dry with paper towels. Cool for 5 minutes.

Blend the sweet potatoes and 2 tablespoons of the butter in a food processor until smooth. Add the Parmesan, chives, and half the egg. Season with salt and freshly ground pepper and allow to cool completely.

Put 2 teaspoons of the mixture in the center of half the wonton wrappers. Brush the edges with the remaining egg, then cover with the remaining wrappers. Press the edges firmly to seal. Using a 2 3/4-inch cookie cutter, cut the ravioli into circles.

Melt the remaining butter in a small saucepan over low heat and cook until golden brown. Remove from the heat.

Cook the ravioli in batches in a large saucepan of boiling water for about 4 minutes. Drain carefully and divide among heated serving plates. Serve the ravioli immediately, drizzled with the butter and sprinkled with the sage and walnuts.

Serves 4

Grilled polenta with shaved fennel salad

2 cups milk
6 oz. polenta
1/3 cup grated Parmesan cheese
1 tablespoon butter
7 oz. fennel bulb
2 cups watercress leaves
1 tablespoon lemon juice
2 tablespoons olive oil
2 tablespoons shaved Parmesan
  cheese

In a heavy-based saucepan, bring the milk and 2 cups water to a boil. Add the polenta and whisk until thoroughly mixed. Reduce the heat as low as possible and simmer for 40 minutes, stirring occasionally to keep it from sticking. Remove from the heat, stir in the Parmesan and butter, and season well. Pour into a greased tray to set (it should be about 3/4 inch thick). When cold, cut into six wedges, brush with a little olive oil, and cook in a hot grilling pan until crisp brown grill marks appear.

Slice the fennel as thinly as possible and chop the fronds. Toss in a bowl with the watercress, lemon juice, oil, and half the Parmesan. Season with salt and black pepper.

Serve the grilled polenta with the fennel salad piled to one side and the remaining shaved Parmesan on top.

Serves 6

Quick mushrooms with red curry sauce

2 cups coconut cream
2 teaspoons red curry paste
  (see Note)
2 teaspoons finely chopped
  lemongrass, white part only
1/2 cup vegetable stock
1 cup coconut milk
2 teaspoons mushroom soy sauce
1 1/2 tablespoons brown sugar
3 fresh kaffir lime leaves
1 tablespoon lime juice
14 oz. assorted mushrooms (shiitake,
  oyster, enoki, button)
2 tablespoons cilantro leaves
3 tablespoons torn Thai basil

Place the coconut cream in a wok, bring to a boil, and cook over high heat for 2–3 minutes. Add the curry paste and chopped lemongrass and cook, stirring continuously, for 3–4 minutes or until fragrant.

Reduce the heat to medium and add the stock, coconut milk, soy sauce, brown sugar, lime leaves, and lime juice. Cook, stirring, for 3–4 minutes or until the sugar has dissolved. Stir in the assorted mushrooms and cook for 3–4 minutes or until tender.

Remove from the heat, stir in the cilantro and basil, and serve with steamed rice.

Serves 4

Note: For a vegetarian meal, make sure the curry paste you use does not contain shrimp paste.

Tofu with chili relish and cashews

Chili relish
1/3 cup peanut oil
12 red Asian shallots, chopped
8 garlic cloves, chopped
8 long red chilies, chopped
2 red peppers, chopped
1 tablespoon tamarind concentrate
1 tablespoon soy sauce
1/2 cup brown sugar

2 tablespoons kecap manis
1 tablespoon peanut oil
6 scallions, cut into 1 1/4-inch lengths
1 lb. 10 oz. silken firm tofu, cut into
   1 1/4-inch cubes
3/4 cup fresh Thai basil
2/3 cup roasted salted cashews

To make the relish, heat half the oil in a frying pan. Add the shallots and garlic and cook over medium heat for 2 minutes. Transfer to a food processor, add the chili and red peppers, and process until smooth. Heat the remaining oil in the pan, add the shallot mixture, and cook over medium heat for 2 minutes. Stir in the tamarind, soy sauce, and sugar and cook for 20 minutes.

Place 2–3 tablespoons of the relish with the kecap manis in a bowl and mix. Heat the oil in a wok over high heat and swirl to coat. Add the scallions, cook for 30 seconds, then remove. Add the tofu and stir-fry for 1 minute, then add the relish and kecap manis mixture. Cook for about 3 minutes or until the tofu is coated and heated through. Return the scallions to the wok, add the basil and cashews, and cook until the basil has wilted.

Serves 4

Asparagus pie

1 lb. 12 oz. fresh asparagus
1½ tablespoons butter
½ teaspoon chopped thyme
1 shallot, chopped
1 large sheet prepared piecrust
⅓ cup cream
2 tablespoons grated Parmesan
  cheese
1 egg
pinch of ground nutmeg
1 egg, extra, lightly beaten

Trim the asparagus spears to 4 inches and cut any thick spears in half lengthwise. Heat the butter in a large frying pan over medium heat and add the asparagus, thyme, and shallot. Add a tablespoon of water and season with salt and pepper. Cook, stirring, for 3 minutes or until the asparagus is tender.

Preheat the oven to 400°F and grease an 8½-inch, fluted springform pan. Roll the piecrust out to a ⅛-inch-thick circle with a diameter of about 12 inches. Line the springform pan and trim the piecrust using kitchen scissors, leaving about 3 inches above the top of the pan. Arrange half the asparagus in one direction across the bottom of the pan. Cover with the remaining asparagus, running in the opposite direction.

Combine the cream, Parmesan, egg, and nutmeg and season to taste with salt and pepper. Pour over the asparagus. Fold the piecrust over the filling, forming loose pleats. Brush with beaten egg and bake in the center of the oven for 25 minutes or until golden.

Serves 6

Tomato tarte tatin

12 Roma tomatoes
4 tablespoons olive oil
3 red onions, finely sliced
2 garlic cloves, finely sliced
1 tablespoon balsamic vinegar
1 teaspoon brown sugar
1/4 cup finely shredded basil
2 1/4 oz. goat cheese
1 sheet frozen puff pastry, thawed

Preheat the oven to 300°F. Cut a cross in the base of each tomato. Cover the tomatoes with boiling water for 30 seconds, then plunge into cold water. Peel the skins away, then cut the tomatoes in half lengthwise and season to taste. Place the tomatoes cut-side up on a rack on a baking tray. Cook in the oven for 3 hours.

Heat 2 tablespoons of oil in a heavy-based saucepan, add the onions, and cook over very low heat, stirring often, for 1 hour or until caramelized.

When the tomatoes are ready, remove from the oven and increase the oven temperature to 400°F.

In an 8-inch, ovenproof frying pan, heat the remaining olive oil over medium heat. Add the garlic, vinegar, sugar, and 1 tablespoon water and heat until the sugar dissolves. Remove from the heat. Arrange the tomatoes in concentric circles, cut-side up, in one layer. Top with the onions, basil, and crumbled goat cheese. Cover with the puff pastry, trim the edges, and tuck the pastry down the side of the pan around the tomatoes. Bake for 25–30 minutes or until the pastry is golden. Invert the tart onto a plate, cool to room temperature, and serve.

Serves 4

Ravioli with roasted red pepper sauce

6 red peppers
1 lb. 6 oz. ravioli
2 tablespoons olive oil
3 garlic cloves, crushed
2 leeks, thinly sliced
1 tablespoon chopped oregano
2 teaspoons brown sugar
1 cup hot vegetable or chicken stock

Cut the peppers into large pieces, removing the seeds and membranes. Cook, skin-side up, under a hot broiler until the skin blackens and blisters. Cool in a plastic bag, then peel away the skin.

Cook the pasta in a large saucepan of boiling water until al dente.

Meanwhile, heat the olive oil in a frying pan and cook the garlic and leeks over medium heat for 3–4 minutes or until softened. Add the oregano and brown sugar and stir for 1 minute.

Place the pepper and leek mixture in a food processor or blender, season with salt and pepper, and process until combined. Add the stock and process until smooth. Drain the pasta and return to the saucepan. Gently toss the sauce through the ravioli over low heat until warmed through. Divide among four serving bowls and serve immediately.

Serves 4

Zucchini omelette

6 tablespoons butter
3 medium zucchini (14 oz.), sliced
1 tablespoon finely chopped basil
pinch of ground nutmeg
8 eggs, lightly beaten

Melt half the butter in a nonstick, 9-inch frying pan. Add the zucchini slices and cook over medium heat for 8 minutes or until lightly golden. Stir in the basil and nutmeg, season with salt and pepper, and cook for 30 seconds. Transfer to a bowl and keep warm.

Wipe out the pan, return it to the heat, and melt the remaining butter. Lightly season the eggs and pour into the pan. Stir gently over high heat. Stop stirring when the mixture begins to set. Reduce the heat and lift the edge with a fork to keep it from catching. Shake the pan from side to side to prevent the omelette from sticking. When it is almost set but still runny on the surface, spread the zucchini down the center. Using a spatula, fold the omelette over and slide onto a plate. Serve immediately.

Serves 4

Sides

Honey-roasted vegetables

4 tablespoons butter
2 tablespoons honey
4 thyme sprigs
3 carrots, peeled and cut into chunks
2 parsnips, peeled and cut into chunks
1 medium orange sweet potato (8 oz.), peeled and cut into chunks
1 medium white sweet potato (8 oz.), peeled and cut into chunks
8 small pickling onions, peeled
8 Jerusalem artichokes, peeled
1 garlic head

Preheat the oven to 400°F. Melt the butter in a large, ovenproof baking dish over medium heat. Add the honey and thyme and stir. Remove from the heat and add the carrots, parsnip, sweet potatoes, onions, and Jerusalem artichokes. Season well with salt and pepper and toss gently so they are coated with the honey butter.

Trim the base of the garlic and wrap in foil. Add to the baking dish and place in the oven for 1 hour, turning the vegetables occasionally so they caramelize evenly. When cooked, remove the foil from the garlic and pop the cloves from their skins. Add to the other vegetables and serve.

Serves 4

Mushrooms with sticky balsamic syrup

⅓ cup olive oil
1 lb. 10 oz. baby button mushrooms
2 large garlic cloves, finely chopped
3 tablespoons brown sugar, firmly
  packed
¼ cup balsamic vinegar
1 tablespoon thyme leaves

Heat the oil in a large, heavy-based, nonstick frying pan. Add the button mushrooms and cook over high heat for 5 minutes or until slightly softened and golden. Season the mushrooms with salt while they are cooking.

Add the garlic and cook for 1 minute. Stir in the brown sugar, vinegar, and 1 tablespoon water and boil for 5 minutes or until reduced by one-third. Season to taste with pepper.

Arrange the mushrooms on a serving plate. Reduce the remaining liquid for 1 minute or until thick and syrupy. Pour over the mushrooms and garnish with the thyme.

Serves 4

Carrots with coconut, ginger, and chili

2 lb. 4 oz. carrots, peeled and cut
    into thick batons
2¼-oz. block of creamed coconut
1 garlic clove, crushed
2 teaspoons grated fresh ginger
2 green chilies, seeded and
    chopped
1 teaspoon ground coriander
1 teaspoon ground cumin
1 teaspoon soy sauce
1 teaspoon chopped lime zest
1 tablespoon lime juice
1 teaspoon brown sugar
3 tablespoons peanut oil
2 tablespoons chopped cilantro
    leaves
lime wedges, to serve

Preheat the oven to 400°F. Bring a large saucepan of water to a boil, blanch the carrots for 5 minutes, then drain well.

Grate the creamed coconut and mix with 2–3 tablespoons of hot water to form a paste. Stir in the garlic, ginger, chili, coriander, cumin, soy sauce, lime zest, lime juice, and brown sugar. Add the carrots and toss to combine.

Pour the peanut oil into a large, shallow-sided roasting pan and heat in the oven for 5 minutes. Toss the carrots in the hot oil, then roast in the oven for 5 minutes. Reduce the heat to 350°F and roast for another 20 minutes or until crisp and golden. Sprinkle with the cilantro leaves and serve with lime wedges.

Serves 6

Baked onions stuffed with goat cheese and sun-dried tomatoes

6 large onions
1/4 cup extra-virgin olive oil
1 garlic clove, crushed
3 1/2 oz. sun-dried tomatoes, finely chopped
1/3 cup fresh white bread crumbs
1 tablespoon chopped parsley
2 teaspoons chopped thyme
3 1/2 oz. mild soft goat cheese, crumbled
1/2 cup Parmesan cheese, grated
1 egg
1 cup vegetable or chicken stock
1 tablespoon butter

Preheat the oven to 350°F. Peel the onions, cut a slice off the top, and reserve. Using a spoon, scrape out a cavity almost to the base of the onion, leaving a hole to stuff.

Blanch the onions in a large saucepan of boiling water for 5 minutes, then drain. Heat 2 tablespoons of oil in a small frying pan and cook the garlic for 3 minutes or until soft. Add the tomatoes, bread crumbs, and herbs and cook for 1 minute. Remove from the heat and add the goat cheese and Parmesan. Season with salt and pepper and stir in the egg.

Stuff the mixture into each onion cavity. Arrange the onions in a large, ceramic, ovenproof baking dish. Pour the stock around the onions and drizzle with the remaining oil. Cover with foil and bake for 45 minutes, basting from time to time. Remove the foil for the last 10 minutes of cooking.

Remove the onions to a serving plate and, over medium heat, simmer the remaining stock for 5–8 minutes or until reduced by half and syrupy. Reduce the heat and whisk in the butter. The sauce should be smooth and glossy. Season to taste and spoon over the onions.

Serves 6

Snake beans stir-fried with Thai basil, garlic, and chili

3 tablespoons soy sauce
¼ cup vegetable or chicken stock
2 tablespoons vegetable oil
1 teaspoon red curry paste
1 red Asian shallot, finely chopped
3 garlic cloves, finely sliced
1 small red chili, seeds removed, sliced
1 lb. 2 oz. snake beans, cut diagonally into 3-inch lengths (see Note)
⅓ cup Thai basil leaves

Combine the soy sauce, stock, and ¼ cup water and set aside.

Heat a wok over high heat, add the vegetable oil, red curry paste, shallot, garlic, and chili, and stir-fry until fragrant. Add the snake beans and cook for 5 minutes. Stir in the sauce and cook, tossing gently, until the beans are tender. Remove from the heat and season well. Stir in half the basil and sprinkle the rest on top as a garnish. Serve immediately.

Serves 4

Note: Snake beans are long, thin, dark green beans and are also known as Chinese beans. Look for them in Asian markets.

Rosemary and garlic roasted potatoes

8 medium potatoes (3 lb. 5 oz.),
  peeled and cut into large chunks
⅓ cup olive oil
12 garlic cloves, root end trimmed,
  skins left on
2 tablespoons rosemary leaves

Preheat the oven to 400°F. Cook the potatoes in a large saucepan of boiling salted water for 10 minutes or until just tender. Drain in a colander and let rest for 5 minutes so that they dry slightly.

Meanwhile, pour the olive oil into a large roasting tray and heat in the oven for 5 minutes. Add the potatoes to the tray (they should sizzle in the hot oil), add the garlic and rosemary, and season well with salt and pepper. Roast, stirring occasionally, so they cook evenly, for about 1 hour or until golden and crisp. Serve with the roasted garlic cloves popped from their skins and the rosemary leaves.

Serves 4–6

Pepperonata

3 red peppers
3 yellow peppers
2 tablespoons olive oil
1 large red onion, thinly sliced
3 large fresh tomatoes, finely
  chopped
1 tablespoon sugar
2 tablespoons balsamic vinegar
2 garlic cloves, finely chopped
¼ cup Italian parsley, chopped

Slice the red and yellow peppers into ¾-inch-wide strips. Heat the oil in a large, heavy-based frying pan and cook the onion over low heat for 5 minutes or until softened. Add the pepper strips and cook for another 5 minutes. Add the tomatoes and cook, covered, over low–medium heat for 10 minutes or until the vegetables are soft. Remove the lid and simmer for another 2 minutes.

Stir in the sugar and vinegar. Place in a serving bowl and sprinkle the garlic and parsley on top. Season with salt and freshly ground black pepper.

Serves 4

Baked sweet potatoes with saffron and pine nut butter

5 medium white sweet potatoes
  (2 lb. 4 oz.)
2 tablespoons vegetable oil
1 tablespoon milk
pinch of saffron threads
1/2 cup unsalted butter, softened
1/4 cup pine nuts, toasted
2 tablespoons finely chopped
  parsley
2 garlic cloves, crushed

Preheat the oven to 350°F. Peel the sweet potatoes and chop into large chunks. Toss to coat with oil. Place them on a baking tray, cover with foil, and roast for 20 minutes.

Warm the milk, add the saffron, and leave to infuse for 5 minutes. Put the butter, milk mixture, pine nuts, parsley, and garlic in a food processor and pulse to combine. Be careful not to overprocess; the nuts should still have some texture. Place a sheet of plastic wrap on the countertop, put the butter in the center, and roll up to form a neat log, about 1 1/2 inches in diameter. Refrigerate the butter for 30 minutes.

Remove the foil from the potatoes and roast, uncovered, for another 30 minutes or until they are cooked through (test for doneness by piercing with a knife). Bring the butter to room temperature, unwrap, cut into 1/2-inch slices, and return to the refrigerator to keep cold.

Arrange the butter slices over the sweet potatoes, season with salt and ground black pepper, and serve.

Serves 4–6

Grilled eggplant with fresh lemon pesto

2 large eggplants, cut into ½-inch
 slices, or 8 baby eggplants, halved
 lengthwise
⅔ cup extra-virgin olive oil
2 cups basil leaves
1 cup parsley
⅓ cup pine nuts, toasted
1–2 garlic cloves, to taste
⅓ cup grated Parmesan cheese
grated zest of 1 lemon
¼ cup lemon juice

Brush both sides of the eggplant slices with 2 tablespoons of extra-virgin olive oil. Heat a grilling pan until hot and cook the eggplant slices for 3 minutes or until golden and cooked through on both sides. If you are using baby eggplants, grill only on the cut side and then finish cooking them by placing in a 400°F oven for 5–8 minutes or until soft. Cover the eggplant slices to keep them warm.

Place the basil, parsley, pine nuts, garlic, Parmesan, lemon zest, and lemon juice in a food processor and blend together. Slowly add the remaining olive oil and process until the mixture forms a smooth paste. Season with salt and freshly ground black pepper.

Stack the eggplant slices on a platter, drizzling some pesto between each layer. Serve immediately.

Serves 4–6

Braised red cabbage

4 tablespoons butter
1 onion, chopped
2 garlic cloves, crushed
2 lb. red cabbage, sliced
2 green apples, peeled, cored, and diced
4 garlic cloves
1/4 teaspoon nutmeg
1 fresh bay leaf
2 juniper berries
1 cinnamon stick
1/3 cup red wine
2 1/2 tablespoons red-wine vinegar
2 tablespoons brown sugar
1 tablespoon red currant jelly
2 cups vegetable or chicken stock

Preheat the oven to 300°F. Heat 3 tablespoons of butter in a large casserole dish, add the onion and garlic, and cook over medium heat for 5 minutes. Add the cabbage and cook for another 10 minutes, stirring frequently.

Add the apples, cloves, nutmeg, bay leaf, juniper berries, and cinnamon stick to the dish. Pour in the red wine and cook for 5 minutes, then add the red-wine vinegar, brown sugar, red currant jelly, and stock. Bring to a boil, then cover and cook in the oven for 2 hours.

After 2 hours of cooking, check the liquid level—there should be only about 1/2 cup left. Stir in the remaining butter, season well with salt and pepper, and serve.

Serves 4–6

Zucchini with mint and feta

6 zucchini
1 tablespoon olive oil
2½ oz. feta cheese, crumbled
1 teaspoon finely grated lemon zest
½ teaspoon chopped garlic
1 tablespoon lemon juice
1 tablespoon extra-virgin olive oil
2 tablespoons shredded mint
2 tablespoons shredded parsley

Slice each zucchini lengthwise into four thick batons. Heat the olive oil in a heavy-based, nonstick frying pan and cook the zucchini over medium heat for 3–4 minutes or until just tender and lightly golden. Arrange on a serving plate.

Crumble the feta over the zucchini. Mix the lemon zest, garlic, and lemon juice in a small cup. Whisk in the extra-virgin olive oil with a fork until well combined, then pour the dressing over the zucchini. Top with the mint and parsley and season with salt and pepper. Serve warm.

Serves 4

Jerusalem artichokes roasted with red wine and garlic

1 lb. 12 oz. Jerusalem artichokes
1 tablespoon lemon juice
2 tablespoons red wine
2 tablespoons olive oil
1 tablespoon tamari
2 garlic cloves, crushed
dash of hot pepper sauce
2 tablespoons vegetable stock
2 tablespoons chopped parsley

Preheat the oven to 400°F. Scrub the artichokes well, then cut them in half lengthwise and place in a bowl of water mixed with the lemon juice.

Combine the red wine, olive oil, tamari, garlic, hot pepper sauce, and stock in a baking tray. Drain the artichoke halves and dry them with paper towels. Place in the baking tray and toss all the ingredients together. Season with salt and freshly ground black pepper.

Bake, covered, for 40 minutes or until tender, then uncover and bake for another 5 minutes or until the juices have formed a reduced glaze. Remove from the oven and toss with the parsley before serving.

Serves 4

Potato packages

1 lb. 9 oz. baby potatoes, halved
2 tablespoons butter, cut into small
   cubes
1 tablespoon thyme sprigs
6 garlic cloves, unpeeled
2 tablespoons olive oil
sea salt, to serve

Preheat the oven to 400°F. Cut two pieces of baking parchment, each 20 inches long. Place half of the potatoes in a single layer on one piece of parchment and sprinkle with half of the butter, half of the thyme, and three cloves of garlic. Drizzle with 1 tablespoon of olive oil. Bring the long edges of the parchment together and fold over twice. Fold over the short edges so that the potatoes are sealed within the paper, and place the packages on a baking tray with the folded side facing down.

Repeat with the remaining ingredients to form a second potato package. Bake for 1 hour 10 minutes or until the potatoes are tender (test for doneness by piercing with a knife). Serve sprinkled with sea salt.

Serves 4

Creamed spinach

3 lb. 5 oz. spinach
2 teaspoons butter
1 garlic clove, crushed
¼ teaspoon freshly grated nutmeg
⅓ cup heavy cream
1 tablespoon grated Parmesan
   cheese

Remove the tough ends from the spinach stalks and wash the leaves well. Shake to remove any excess water from the leaves, but do not dry completely.

Melt the butter in a large frying pan. Add the crushed garlic and the spinach, season with nutmeg, salt, and pepper, and cook over medium heat until the spinach is just wilted. Remove from the heat and place the spinach in a sieve. Press down well to squeeze out all of the excess moisture. Transfer to a chopping board, and using a sharp knife, chop the spinach finely.

Pour the cream into the frying pan and heat gently. Add the spinach to the pan and stir until warmed through. Arrange the spinach on a serving dish and sprinkle with the Parmesan.

Serves 4–6

Roasted beets with horseradish cream

8 beets
2 tablespoons olive oil
2 teaspoons honey
1½ tablespoons creamed
 horseradish
½ cup sour cream
chopped parsley, to garnish

Preheat the oven to 400°F. Scrub and peel the beets, trim the ends, and cut into quarters. Place the oil and honey in a small bowl and mix well. Season with salt and freshly ground black pepper.

Place the beets on a large square of foil and drizzle with the honey mixture, coating them well. Enclose the beets loosely in the foil. Bake for 1 hour or until the beets are tender when pierced with a skewer.

Meanwhile, combine the horseradish and sour cream and season lightly with salt and pepper. Once the beets are cooked, remove from the oven and leave in the foil for 5 minutes. Remove from the foil and serve with a generous dollop of the horseradish cream and garnish with the parsley.

Serves 4

Deep-fried Parmesan carrots

1 lb. 2 oz. baby carrots
1/2 cup all-purpose flour
2 teaspoons ground cumin
2 eggs
3 cups fine fresh white bread crumbs
1 tablespoon chopped parsley
2/3 cup finely grated Parmesan cheese
vegetable oil, for deep-frying

Trim the leafy carrot tops, leaving about 3/4 inch, and wash the carrots. Bring a large saucepan of water to a boil, add 1 teaspoon of salt, and cook the carrots for 5 minutes or until tender (test for doneness with a metal skewer). Drain, dry well with paper towels, and leave to cool.

Sift the flour and cumin onto a sheet of waxed paper, then beat the eggs together in a wide, shallow bowl. Combine the bread crumbs, parsley, and Parmesan and season with salt and pepper. Roll the carrots in the flour, then the eggs, and finally the bread crumbs. For an extra-crispy coating, repeat this process.

Fill a deep, heavy-based saucepan one-third full of oil and heat until a cube of bread dropped into the oil browns in 20 seconds. Deep-fry the carrots in batches until golden and crisp. Serve immediately.

Serves 6

Green beans with feta and tomatoes

1 tablespoon olive oil
1 onion, chopped
2 garlic cloves, crushed
1½ tablespoons chopped oregano
½ cup white wine
15-oz. can diced tomatoes
1½ cups green beans, trimmed
1 tablespoon balsamic vinegar
7 oz. feta cheese, cut into ½-inch cubes

Heat the oil in a saucepan, add the onion, and cook over medium heat for 3–5 minutes or until soft. Add the garlic and half the oregano and cook for another minute. Pour in the white wine and cook for 3 minutes or until reduced by one-third.

Stir in the diced tomatoes and cook, uncovered, for 10 minutes. Add the beans and cook, covered, for another 10 minutes.

Stir in the balsamic vinegar, feta, and remaining oregano. Season with salt and pepper and serve.

Serves 4

Orange sweet potato wedges with tangy cumin mayonnaise

2 1/2 tablespoons olive oil
6 medium orange sweet potatoes
   (2 lb. 4 oz.), peeled and cut into
   2 1/2-inch-long wedges
3/4 cup mayonnaise
1/4 cup lime juice
1 teaspoon honey
1 heaping tablespoon roughly
   chopped cilantro
1 1/2 teaspoons ground cumin

Preheat the oven to 400°F. Place the olive oil in a large roasting pan and heat in the oven for 5 minutes.

Place the sweet potatoes in the pan in a single layer, season with salt and pepper, and bake for 35 minutes, turning occasionally.

While the sweet potatoes are cooking, place the mayonnaise, lime juice, honey, cilantro, and cumin in a food processor and blend until smooth.

Drain the wedges on crumpled paper towels and serve with the tangy cumin mayonnaise on the side.

Serves 4

Cauliflower pilaf

1 cup basmati rice
2 tablespoons olive oil
1 large onion, thinly sliced
¼ teaspoon cardamom seeds
½ teaspoon ground turmeric
1 cinnamon stick
1 teaspoon cumin seeds
¼ teaspoon cayenne pepper
2 cups vegetable or chicken stock
1 head cauliflower (1 lb. 12 oz.),
   trimmed and cut into florets
⅓ cup chopped cilantro leaves

Put the rice in a sieve and rinse under cold running water. Set aside to drain.

Heat the oil in a saucepan with a tightly fitting lid. Cook the onion over medium heat, stirring frequently, for 5 minutes or until soft and lightly golden. Add the spices and cook, stirring, for 1 minute.

Add the rice to the pan and stir to coat in the spices. Add the stock and cauliflower, stirring to combine.

Cover with the lid and bring to a boil. Reduce the heat to very low and cook for 15 minutes or until the rice and cauliflower are tender and all the stock has been absorbed.

Fold the cilantro through the rice and serve immediately.

Serves 6

Fennel with walnut parsley crust

2 tablespoons lemon juice
9 small fennel bulbs, halved
  lengthwise
1 teaspoon fennel seeds
1 cup grated Parmesan cheese
2 cups fresh bread crumbs
1 cup chopped walnuts
1 tablespoon chopped parsley
2 teaspoons lemon zest
2 garlic cloves, chopped
1 cup vegetable or chicken stock
2 tablespoons butter

Bring a large saucepan of water to a boil and add the lemon juice and 1 teaspoon of salt. Add the fennel and cook for 5–10 minutes or until tender, then drain and cool.

Heat a frying pan over medium heat and dry-fry the fennel seeds for 1 minute to release their flavor. Put the seeds in a food processor, then add the Parmesan, bread crumbs, walnuts, parsley, lemon zest, and garlic, and pulse gently to combine. Stir in 2 tablespoons of stock to moisten the mixture.

Place the fennel bulbs, flat-side up, in an ovenproof ceramic dish and top with the stuffing, spreading to completely cover each piece. Pour the remaining stock around the fennel bulbs and top each piece with 1/2 teaspoon of butter. Bake for 25 minutes, basting from time to time, until the top is golden and the fennel bulbs are cooked through. Serve drizzled with the braising juices.

Serves 4

Potato rosti

5 medium waxy (e.g., red) potatoes
 (1 lb. 10 oz.), peeled
1 small onion, finely sliced
2 tablespoons chopped parsley
2 tablespoons butter
2 teaspoons olive oil

Boil the potatoes for 10–15 minutes or until they just begin to soften. Drain, then allow to cool. Grate the potatoes and place in a large bowl with the onion and parsley. Season well with salt and pepper.

Heat the butter and oil in a nonstick frying pan over medium–low heat. When the butter has melted, add the potato mixture to the pan, spreading the mixture out but not pressing too firmly. Cover the pan and cook for 8–10 minutes or until golden and crispy. Halfway through the cooking time, check to ensure the rosti is not burning. Carefully turn by flipping the whole rosti onto a plate, then sliding it, uncooked-side down, back into the pan. Cover and cook for 5 minutes or until golden brown. Cut into four pieces and serve.

Serves 4

Cabbage with leek and mustard seeds

1 tablespoon vegetable oil
2 tablespoons unsalted butter
2 teaspoons black mustard seeds
2 leeks, washed and thinly sliced
3 cups thinly shredded cabbage
1 tablespoon lemon juice
5 tablespoons crème fraîche
2 tablespoons chopped parsley

Heat the oil and butter together, add the mustard seeds, and cook until they start to pop. Add the leeks and cook gently for 5–8 minutes or until softened. Stir in the cabbage and cook over low heat for 4 minutes or until it wilts and softens.

Season the cabbage with salt and pepper. Add the lemon juice and crème fraîche and cook for another minute. Stir in the chopped parsley and serve immediately.

Serves 4–6

Roasted red onions and Roma tomatoes with balsamic vinaigrette

vegetable oil, to brush
8 Roma tomatoes
2 red onions
2 garlic cloves
1½ tablespoons balsamic vinegar
1 teaspoon French mustard
¼ cup extra-virgin olive oil

Preheat the oven to 300°F and lightly brush a baking tray with oil.

Cut the tomatoes into quarters and arrange on the tray. Remove the tops of the onion and peel. Cut each onion into eight wedges and place on the tray with the tomatoes. Place the garlic in the middle of the tray, spaced 2 inches apart, and season all of the vegetables with salt and pepper. Roast for 1 hour.

Arrange the tomatoes and onions on a serving plate. Peel the garlic and crush in a small bowl. Add the balsamic vinegar and mustard to the garlic and, using a small wire whisk, beat in the olive oil, adding it slowly in a thin stream. Season the dressing with salt and pepper and drizzle over the onions and tomatoes. Serve immediately.

Serves 4

Parsnip chips

4 parsnips
vegetable oil, for deep-frying
1/4 teaspoon ground cumin

Trim and peel the parsnips. Using a vegetable peeler, cut them into long, thick strips.

Fill a deep, heavy-based saucepan one-third full of oil and heat until a cube of bread dropped in the oil browns in 15 seconds. Deep-fry the parsnip strips in batches for 1 minute or until they are golden and crisp. Remove from the oil and drain on crumpled paper towels.

Mix 2 teaspoons of salt with the cumin in a small bowl. Put the hot parsnip chips in a large bowl and season with the cumin mixture. Serve immediately.

Serves 4

Gai larn with ginger, lime, and peanuts

1 lb. 5 oz. gai larn (Chinese broccoli)
1½ oz. tamarind pulp
1 small red chili
1 tablespoon peanut oil
2 garlic cloves, finely chopped
1 tablespoon finely grated fresh
  ginger
1 tablespoon sugar
1 tablespoon lime juice
1 teaspoon sesame oil
1 tablespoon roasted unsalted
  peanuts, finely chopped

Trim the ends from the gai larn and slice in half. Place the tamarind in a bowl and add ¼ cup boiling water. Allow to steep for 5 minutes, then strain, discarding the solids.

Slice the chili in half, remove the seeds and membrane, and chop finely. Heat a wok until very hot, add the peanut oil, and swirl it around to coat the wok. Add the gai larn and stir-fry for 2–3 minutes or until wilted. Add the chili, garlic, and ginger and cook for another minute. Add the sugar, lime juice, and 1 tablespoon of tamarind liquid and simmer for 1 minute.

Remove the gai larn to a serving plate and drizzle with the sesame oil. Sprinkle with peanuts and season to taste with salt and pepper.

Serves 4

Brussels sprouts with chestnut and sage butter

2 tablespoons butter, softened
¼ cup peeled, cooked chestnuts, finely chopped (see Note)
1 teaspoon chopped sage
1 lb. 9 oz. Brussels sprouts, trimmed

Put the butter, chopped chestnuts, and sage in a bowl and mix together well. Scrape onto a large piece of waxed paper and shape into a log, using the paper to help shape the butter. Wrap in the paper and refrigerate until firm.

Cook the Brussels sprouts in salted, boiling water for 10–12 minutes or until tender. Drain well. Be careful not to overcook the sprouts or they will become soggy. Cut the chilled butter into thin slices. Toss four of the slices with the sprouts until they are evenly coated in butter, then season well. Arrange the remaining slices on top of the sprouts and serve immediately.

Serves 4

Note: If chestnuts are unavailable, use toasted walnuts instead.

Tagliatelle of root vegetables in spiced cream

4 large carrots
2 large parsnips
iced water
3/4 cup cream
1 garlic clove, crushed
1/3 cup finely grated Parmesan cheese
2 tablespoons chopped chives

Peel the outer skins from the carrots and parsnips, and discard. Peel long, thin strips from the vegetables until you reach the hard cores. Bring a large saucepan of water to a boil, add 1 teaspoon of salt, and blanch the vegetables for 1 minute. Drain, then rinse in a bowl of iced water.

Pour the cream into a saucepan and add the crushed garlic. Stir over medium heat until reduced to about 1/2 cup. Add 2 tablespoons Parmesan and 1 tablespoon chives, then season well with salt and freshly ground black pepper.

Drain the vegetables, then add to the cream and stir gently over medium heat for 2 minutes or until warmed through. Garnish with the remaining Parmesan and chives, and serve.

Serves 4

Mashed carrots
with cumin seeds

6 carrots
1 tablespoon olive oil
2 garlic cloves, finely chopped
1 teaspoon ground turmeric
2 teaspoons finely grated fresh
  ginger
1/4 cup plain yogurt
2 teaspoons prepared harissa
2 tablespoons chopped cilantro
  leaves
2 teaspoons lime juice
1 teaspoon cumin seeds

Peel the carrots and cut into 1-inch chunks. Place them in a large saucepan and cover with cold water. Bring to a boil, then reduce the heat and simmer for 3 minutes. Drain and allow to dry.

Heat the olive oil in a heavy-based, nonstick saucepan. Cook the garlic, ground turmeric, and ginger over medium heat for 1 minute or until fragrant. Add the carrots and cook for 3 minutes. Stir in 1 tablespoon water and cook, covered, over low heat for 10–15 minutes or until the carrots are soft. Transfer the mixture to a bowl and roughly mash.

Add the yogurt, harissa, cilantro, and lime juice to the carrots and stir to combine. Season to taste with salt and freshly ground black pepper.

Heat a heavy-based frying pan, add the cumin seeds, and dry-fry for 1–2 minutes or until fragrant. Sprinkle over the mashed carrots and serve.

Serves 4

Indian-style spinach

2 tablespoons ghee (clarified butter)
  or vegetable oil
1 onion, thinly sliced
2 garlic cloves, finely chopped
2 teaspoons finely grated fresh ginger
1 teaspoon brown mustard seeds
1/2 teaspoon ground cumin
1/4 teaspoon ground coriander
1 teaspoon ground turmeric
1/2 teaspoon garam masala
12 oz. fresh spinach, trimmed
1/4 cup cream
1 tablespoon lemon juice

Heat a wok until very hot. Add the ghee and swirl it around to coat the wok. Stir-fry the onion over medium heat for 2 minutes to soften. Add the garlic, ginger, brown mustard seeds, cumin, coriander, turmeric, and garam masala and cook for 1 minute or until fragrant.

Roughly tear the spinach leaves in half and add to the spice mixture. Cook for 1–2 minutes or until wilted. Add the cream, simmer for 2 minutes, then add the lemon juice and season with salt and freshly ground black pepper. Serve hot.

Serves 4

Squash with chili

1 lb. 12 oz. butternut squash
2 tablespoons vegetable oil
2 garlic cloves, crushed
1 teaspoon grated fresh ginger
2 bird's-eye chilies, finely chopped
1 teaspoon finely grated lime zest
1 tablespoon lime juice
1½ tablespoons light soy sauce
¾ cup vegetable or chicken stock
1 tablespoon soy sauce
1 teaspoon brown sugar
¾ cup cilantro leaves, chopped

Peel the squash, then scoop out the seeds so that you have about 1 lb. 5 oz. of flesh. Cut the flesh into ½-inch cubes.

Heat the oil in a large frying pan or wok over medium heat, add the garlic, ginger, and chili, and stir-fry for 1 minute. Keep moving the garlic and chili around the pan to ensure they don't burn, as this will make them taste bitter. Add the squash, lime zest, lime juice, light soy sauce, stock, soy sauce, and brown sugar, then cover and cook for 10 minutes or until the squash is tender.

Remove the lid and gently stir for 5 minutes or until any remaining liquid has reduced. Gently stir in the chopped cilantro and serve immediately.

Serves 4

Fried green tomatoes with a cornmeal crust

5 medium green (unripe) tomatoes
  (1 lb. 10 oz.)
½ cup all-purpose flour
1½ cups yellow cornmeal
2 teaspoons finely chopped thyme
2 teaspoons finely chopped marjoram
½ cup grated Parmesan cheese
2 eggs, beaten with 1 tablespoon
  water
olive oil, for frying

Preheat the oven to 350°F. Cut the tomatoes into ½-inch slices and season with salt. Season the flour with salt and freshly ground black pepper and place in a shallow bowl. Combine the cornmeal, thyme, marjoram, and Parmesan. Dip the tomato slices in the flour, coating all over, then dip in the beaten egg, followed by the cornmeal mixture. Set the tomatoes aside in a single layer.

Fill a large, heavy-based frying pan with olive oil to ¼ inch deep. Heat over medium heat until a cube of bread dropped in the oil browns in 20 seconds. Reduce the heat a little, then cook the tomato slices in batches for 2–3 minutes each side, or until golden. Remove with tongs and drain on paper towels. Transfer the tomato slices to a plate and keep them warm in the oven while the rest are being cooked. Add more oil to the pan as necessary to maintain the level. Serve hot.

Serves 4–6

Sweet corn with lime and chili butter

4 corncobs
4 tablespoons butter
2 tablespoons olive oil
1 stem lemongrass, bruised and
   cut in half
3 small bird's-eye chilies, seeded
   and finely chopped
2 tablespoons lime zest, finely
   grated
2 tablespoons lime juice
2 tablespoons finely chopped
   cilantro leaves

Remove the skins and silky threads from the corncobs. Wash well, then use a long, sharp knife to cut each cob into 3/4-inch chunks.

Heat the butter and oil in a large saucepan over low heat. Add the lemongrass and braise gently for 5 minutes, then remove from the pan. Add the chili and cook for 2 minutes. Stir in the grated lime zest, lime juice, 3 tablespoons of water, and the corn. Cover and cook, shaking the pan frequently, for 5–8 minutes or until the corn is tender. Season well, then stir in the cilantro and serve hot.

Serves 4

Note: Offer plenty of napkins with this dish, as the corn chunks can be messy to eat.

Index

Index

Index

Index

Laurel Glen Publishing
An imprint of the Advantage Publishers Group
5880 Oberlin Drive, San Diego, CA 92121-4794
www.laurelglenbooks.com

Text, design, photography, and illustrations © Murdoch Books, 2004

All notations of errors or omissions should be addressed to Laurel Glen Publishing, Editorial Department, at the above address. All other correspondence (author inquiries, permissions, and rights) concerning the content of this book should be addressed to Murdoch Books® a division of Murdoch Magazines Pty Ltd, Pier 8/9, 23 Hickson Road, Millers Point NSW 2000, Australia.

NOTE: Those who might be at risk from the effects of salmonella poisoning (the elderly, pregnant women, young children, and those with a compromised immune system) should consult their physician before trying recipes made with raw eggs.

Library of Congress Cataloging-in-Publication Data

Veggie food.
   p. cm.
   Includes index.
   ISBN 1-59223-283-3
   1. Vegetarian Cookery. I. Laurel Glen Publishing.

  TX837.V434 2004
  641.5'656--dc22
                     2004047076

Printed by Sing Cheong Printing Co. Ltd, Hong Kong
1 2 3 4 5   08 07 06 05 04

Editorial Director: Diana Hill
Creative Director: Marylouise Brammer
Photographers: Jared Fowler, Ian Hofstetter
Food Preparation: Michelle Earl, Joanne Kelly
Chief Executive: Juliet Rogers

Editor: Rachel Carter
Designer: Michelle Cutler
Stylists: Jane Collins, Cherise Koch
Production: Monika Paratore
Publisher: Kay Scarlett

You may find cooking times vary depending on the oven you are using. For convection ovens, as a general rule, set the oven temperature 40°F lower than indicated in the recipe.

We have used large eggs in all recipes.